MAKE WAY FOR THE SPIRIT

MAKE WAY FOR THE SPIRIT

MICHAEL J. COLE

HIGHLAND BOOKS

Printed in Great Britain for
HIGHLAND BOOKS
Broadway House, The Broadway,
Crowborough, East Sussex, TN6 1BY
by Richard Clay Ltd., Bungay, Suffolk

To the Fellowship of All Saints', Woodford Wells.
Together we have experienced the renewing work of the Spirit. Sometimes it has been painful, often it has been a great blessing. You have encouraged me, prayed for and with me, taught me and shared with me.

We are still learning, but thank you for sharing the journey so far. May we all make way for the Spirit in our corporate and individual life.

Contents

Introduction

Make Way for the Spirit began life round our kitchen table one Friday lunch-time.

Three years ago, Edward England—who has been a constant source of help and encouragement, a modern day Barnabas—approached me about the possibility of writing a regular question and answer column for *Renewal* magazine. It seemed right to accept, so long as I could work with a team. The team first met in September 1985 and now meets monthly on a Friday lunch-time.

The meal is usually home-made soup—and my wife Stephanie makes the best—some rolls, bread and cheese and fruit, followed by tea or coffee. The fellowship is great. The questions, usually sent in by readers, have been circulated beforehand and the team have thought and prayed and read so that, after further prayer and food, we share and stimulate each other. It is fascinating to see how the contributions differ. I'm busy jotting down additional thoughts and comments and we end with prayer and the washing up. I'm then left to write up the answers. The blemishes are mine, the wisdom is often that of others—and always, we hope, from the Lord.

The team who have shared with me are Stephanie, my wife, and Jane French, a member of our ministry team, Mark Philps, a former colleague now working in the Midlands, and two businessmen who have had experience of various mainline and house church fellowships—Mark Smith and David Blackledge. On two or three occasions we have been augmented by visiting theological college students staying in the parish—like Pam and David.

Jackie Arnold, my untiring secretary, and Jean Skelton, who sells Renewal—and other books and magazines on the church bookstall—have been involved with the typing and checking of the manuscript.

Many of the questions in *Make Way for the Spirit* first appeared in the then bi-monthly but now monthly pages of *Renewal* magazine. Some answers have been revised for this publication. Other questions which I felt needed to be asked and answered have been added. I hope we have produced a little volume which can be put into the hands of many church members around the world and which answers some of the many questions arising in our minds as we make way for the Spirit.

If it happens that these questions and answers provoke other questions, then I hope you will address them to me c/o Renewal Magazine, Broadway House, The Broadway, Crowborough, East Sussex, TN6 1BY, England. Maybe we can enjoy some more home-made soup, and prayer and fellowship around the table on a Friday lunch-time to produce some more answers for the monthly column.

My introduction would not be complete without a further acknowledgement to Edward England. He not only launched the question page column, but also suggested this book. My debt to him is great.

Michael Cole

(Unless otherwise stated, all the Bible references are taken from the New International Version of the Bible, Hodder and Stoughton, 1980.)

1

Renewal and Baptism in the Spirit

What is Renewal?

Renewal seems to be an overworked word with people giving it just the meaning that they want it to have!

Josephine Bax in her book, *The Good Wine*, identifies the different kinds or aspects of renewal about which people speak: charismatic renewal; liturgical renewal; renewal of marriages; renewal through the Cursillo Movement; renewal as it affects the ecumenical movement among the churches; renewal of the political outlook of the churches and its members. Clearly, there are a number of renewal streams flowing in the spiritual wastelands, but the questions we have to ask are: Are all the streams flowing from the same source, and, if so, what and where is this source?

The meaning of renewal

If we go back to our final authority—the Bible—we shall find that the word renewal is used six times in the New Testament (see 2 Corinthians 4:16; Colossians 3:10; Romans 12:2; Titus 3:5; Hebrews 6:6; Ephesians 4:23). As we study the context of each passage carefully, two truths will become abundantly clear about the meaning of renewal.

First, it is something that happens to us. While we have to be willing for renewal to happen, it is not something that we do to our lives or our churches. It is something that God brings about by the Holy Spirit. Secondly, renewal is not updating something that is old, like renewing our car licence, or having more of the same old thing. Rather the word means 'to make completely different', like replacing the worn-out furniture in the sitting-room with something new and exciting. Renewal is about having much more of something different and better. Michael Harper has written in *Glory in the Church* of renewal as 'a fresh quality', adding: 'There is no need for a new church, but the refurbishing of the old, and God's Spirit will do that.'

I quote from *Renewal*, April/May 1986, where Edward England gathered together many quotes and definitions about renewal and what it involved:

- *Repentance:* The Holy Spirit convicting us of sin . . . a turning from the mind of the flesh to the mind of God.
- *Assurance:* Renewal is a journey into the unknown that I used to call God—then one day discovered I had to cry out his name, 'Abba, Father.'
- *Thirst:* Renewal is expectancy, a waiting on the Lord, a deep personal openness to God.
- *Awakening:* Renewal is a release of God's love, of God's power, of God's people . . . an opening up of deep inner springs to the creativity of the Holy Spirit in music, poetry, drama.
- *The Holy Spirit:* Renewal is being filled with the Spirit, a switching from dependence on natural talents to a seeking of God's power . . . being enriched by the fruits of the Spirit and empowered by the gifts of the Spirit.

● *Authority:* Renewal is authority in conflict with demonic powers (Luke 10:19; Acts 1:8).

● *Praise:* Renewal is a recognition that the fundamental work of the Holy Spirit is to glorify Jesus . . . being separate and holy, with a sense of exultant rejoicing.

● *Sharing:* Renewal is showing Jesus to the world . . . a new economic order where men share their goods and possessions, where Jew and Gentile eat together at the Lord's table.

● *The church:* Renewal is a rebirth of the local church, as a continuous process . . . a genuine awakening of the whole people of God.

Renewal is the inward work of God in our lives. It is not necessarily about singing songs from *Songs of Fellowship* instead of *Ancient and Modern*, raising our hands in worship, playing guitars, hugging, clapping and dancing; nor about glorying in dramatic gifts or in signs and wonders.

The picture of renewal

It is often helpful to 'earth' the general truths in a particular event, and there is no event in the Bible that helps me to understand renewal better than Ezekiel's vision in the Valley of Dry Bones (Ezekiel chapter 37). The people who needed renewing were God's people (v.11). They were dry, but not dead. God's great vision for his people had been lost. The valley was the place where once there had been a vision of God's majesty but that had faded.

Renewal is the need of the dry people of God who have lost their vision and are aware of their powerlessness. Renewal must not therefore be confused with regeneration, which is the need of the unconverted, nor with revival, which is the sovereign work of God's grace and spirit; nor should it be equated with resurrection or even with restoration—often akin to renewal but related to the bringing in of the Kingdom of God; and it is not synonymous with human re-organisation.

The vision that God gave to Ezekiel teaches us that renewal comes about as a result of God's work with man's co-operation (v.3). It is God who asks the question, 'Can these bones live?' God knows what he will do through his power, but he is testing Ezekiel as to what he believes God can and will do. Has the prophet enough faith to believe God can and will work?

God works through three agents: the word of God (v.4); the Spirit of God (vs.1, 5, 6, 8, 9, 10, 14); the servant of God (vs. 4, 9). So often God brings renewal into a fellowship or church through his faithful servant(s) who will bring us back, on the one hand, to the truth of the Bible and, on the other, to the availability of the power and ministry of the Holy Spirit. The word that is used for the Spirit—*ruach*—can be translated as either a gentle breeze or a stormy wind—which corresponds to different experiences of renewal. There can be the quiet gracious work of the Spirit in one person's life, while another person may be knocked over and overwhelmed with an experience of him: he knows what is right for each of us.

The renewal movement is not the work of man renewing the church by changing the outward structures, introducing a new liturgy and passing resolutions; it is the work of God's Spirit renewing inwardly the church of Jesus.

We also discover from this same passage the attractive results of renewal in Ezekiel's experience.

● A new experience of the Lord: 'You shall know that I am the Lord' (v.6). One church has expressed their understanding of charismatic renewal in these words: 'The charismatic experience is nothing other than the experience of the living God . . . The church, as we have known it, has functioned so long subnormally that, were it ever to become normal, it would seem abnormal.'

● Service and ministry. Instead of the bones being concerned with survival, they are outgoing in service to others (v.10). The great army stands upon its feet. I'm always thrilled with that picture. This is what God is bringing about throughout the world as he renews his church by the power of the Spirit—a power that is primarily for mission and not for miracles.

● Glory being brought to the Lord (vs.13–14). The people know that the Lord has acted in this way through the work of his Spirit.

● The coming together of the separate parts of the body of Christ in unity and fellowship (vs.14–15). They now serve under one king.

It is thrilling to compare the start of this vision, with the end. A valley full of dry bones becoming a mighty army, standing upon its feet ready for the work to which God calls it.

The desire for renewal

Faced with a similar attractive possibility today, you would expect that all of us would long to know the renewing work of God's Spirit. Sadly, we react in different ways. Some of us are fearful, others are sceptical or don't see the need or have all sorts of questions—or excuses—to put off facing the matter of renewal in our own lives.

I hope that some of the answers given in this book in response to other people's questions may bring reassurance to the uncertain. But may I point those who long to move forward in renewal to Jesus's promise in John 7:37–39: 'On the last and greatest day of the Feast, Jesus stood and said in a loud voice, "If a man is thirsty, let him come to me and drink. Whoever believes in me, as the Scripture has said, streams of living waters will flow from within him." By this he meant the Spirit whom those who believed in him were later to receive. Up to that time the Spirit had not been given, since Jesus had not yet been glorified.'

Renewal is the result of the Spirit of Jesus flowing out from within a person, not only refreshing his thirsty life but also blessing all those around. Such renewal is available to those who go on being thirsty, coming to Jesus, and drinking, for then the Holy Spirit will go on flowing out from within. Renewal is not a goal to be reached, nor a plateau on which to stand, but a spring to be found; and from that spring of spiritual life and power we go on drinking to the glory of Jesus and the blessing of others.

What place does repentance have in renewal?

The short reply to this question is, 'A central place'. Repentance is at the heart of renewal. Maybe asking three other related questions, will help us to understand why repentance is so important.

What is repentance?
Essentially repentance means changing our minds and turning from one way of life to another. For example, the Thessalonians turned to God from idols to serve the living and true God (1 Thessalonians 1:9). Peter made

the same point—and linked it with renewal—when he preached, 'Repent, and turn to God, so that your sins may be wiped out, that times of refreshing may come from the Lord' (Acts 3:19).

Also repentance is often vitally linked with the rule and lordship of God: 'Repent for the kingdom of God is at hand' (Matthew 3:2). 'We will not have this man to reign over us' (Luke 19:14) demonstrates the opposite attitude.

Unless there is repentance, there will be increasing spiritual blindness. Jesus often warned of the dangers of an unrepentant heart (Matthew 11:20; 12:38). So repentance is part of our response in restoring a right relationship with God and submitting to his rule in our lives. That surely is at the heart of renewal. But let's ask a second question.

Who has to repent?
From a study of the Bible it is clear that there are three groups of people mentioned and we are all included in at least one of them!

Everyone needs to repent at conversion. Repentance and faith are at the heart of the Christian life, and there are many Scriptures that make this point (Matthew 9:13; Luke 15:7; Acts 2:38; 17:30–31; 20:21; 26:20). If we have turned to Christ, without also turning from sin, the world and our previous non-Christian way of life, we should not be surprised at finding that things are hard going, spiritually.

Individual Christians within the fellowship from time to time need to repent. I'm sure we all know those times when we have to admit the wrongs we have done or the good we have not done, and to ask the Lord to restore us. Our Church of England prayer book ser-vices build this provision into our regular Sunday worship. When we repent, we know the fresh flow of the stream of the Spirit of Jesus within our lives.

Churches are also called to corporate repentance. The ascended Christ challenged the churches of Asia Minor (Revelation chapters 2–3) to repent of immorality, coldness of heart, unbelief and lack of love (see especially Revelation 2:5; 2:16; 3:3). It was as those churches turned away from what was displeasing to the Lord, and turned again to him in obedience that they knew the blessing and approval of the head of the Church.

Although a number of our congregation had entered personally into renewal and were growing in the life of the Spirit, it was not until we, as a church, repented of our selfishness, pride and independent spirit, and came to the point of acknowledging, in practice, that Jesus was lord of our church, that we really began to move forward effectively. We still have to watch that we don't fall back into complacency and pride and that we continue to ensure that Jesus is lord. But, as a church, we needed to repent of those wrong attitudes, and allow him truly to be the head of the Church.

How do I—or we, as a church—repent?
Repentance is an act of the will. Are you willing to turn from wrong attitudes and actions? Do you know of what you have to repent? It is important that you know the answers to these questions. We have to be willing. Often we may feel completely incapable of changing, but the marvellous truth is that Jesus will help us change, if we are willing to change. If you turn to Acts 5:31 and 11:18 you will find that the Lord enables us to do what he commands us to do. He will give repentance to those who seek it.

Repentance is often very practical. We turn from

whatever the Lord has indicated, and we turn afresh to him. It is not primarily changing one activity programme for another. It is changing our attitude from self-centredness to Christ-centredness. We stop running our lives, and we begin—or continue—to allow the Lord to be in charge. When that happens—there's renewal.

Should renewal affect social and political issues today?

The simple answer is, 'Yes.' The renewing work of the Spirit of God should overflow to affect social and political issues today.

If you look at the context of Ephesians 4:30 or the events surrounding the tragic deaths of Ananias and Sapphira in Acts chapter 5, you will find that their wrong relationship with the Spirit was linked with wrong attitudes towards money, work, sex and speech. They were affected socially, because they were in error spiritually.

Secondly (see Acts 11:28ff.), material relief supplies (the first TEAR fund?) were organised for the Christians at Jerusalem as the result of a prophecy in the power of the Spirit; and, in Ezekiel chapter 37, the renewing of God's people was to affect the country politically. The familiar words of Isaiah 61:1 and Luke 4:18ff.—'The Spirit of the Lord is upon me . . .'—illustrate this same truth that the outworking of the ministry of the Spirit cannot and must not be boxed up into watertight compartments but should flow out and influence every part of our lives.

This is the lovely testimony of some today. For example, Jackie Pullinger is ministering to the drug addicts and young people in the walled city of Hong

Kong. The Prison Christian Fellowship is working among an often neglected section of the community.

The Spirit who renews is also the Spirit who longs to reach out to all sorts and conditions of people in mission. We should therefore be ready for God to be calling us, as churches and individuals, to respond to social and political issues today, as a further outworking of God's renewing activity.

Do I have to be renewed to minister to other people?

People today use the term minister to mean praying for people after a service or meeting needs, whether this involves visiting, comforting or whatever. It is vital that we see what the New Testament teaches about this. The key passage is 1 Peter 4:10–11: 'Each one should use whatever gift he has received to serve others, faithfully administering God's grace in its various forms. If anyone speaks, he should do it as one speaking the very words of God. If anyone serves, he should do it with the strength God provides, so that in all things God may be praised through Jesus Christ.'

Ministry, therefore, covers anything from speaking to serving: meeting the needs of another; so it could include things like making sure the church newsletter is delivered regularly to a house-bound church member; keeping in touch by letter with a student away from home or a missionary serving overseas; praying for a person's healing; welcoming someone at the church door.

In every instance, the New Testament makes it clear that if the task is to be carried out to the glory of God and the blessing of others, it must be done by those who are walking in the Spirit and not in the flesh. That, after all, is the normal standard expected of New Testament Christians. They were taught to allow the Holy Spirit to go on filling them. They were to be renewed in mind and spirit day by day. Renewal by the Spirit is the expected standard, not the extraordinary experience (see Romans 12:1; 2 Corinthians 4:16). Unless our lives are available to God and open to the Holy Spirit, then we will not walk with the fragrance of the Spirit's fruit and grace or serve and minister in the power of the Spirit's gifts. That applies not only to prayer ministry to one another, but also to every way in which members of the body are called to serve the Lord.

Why do some Christians speak about renewal, while others refer to restoration in the church? Do they mean the same thing?

'Probably not,' is the short answer. The question touches on some very important and sensitive issues between Christians, and really warrants a much longer answer than space permits me to give here. But perhaps we can understand the issues better if we ask three simple questions.

Where are people 'coming from'? The past background is important. Those who talk about renewal often mean the personal spiritual renewal of members of traditional main-line churches and denominations. Those who speak of restoration have often come from an independent background, are suspicious of institutional Christianity, and believe that a radical restoration of the corporate life of the church is called for. This different

starting point is reflected in the publication of *Renewal*
and *Restoration*—two Christian monthly magazines.

What are people looking for? Those who work for the
restoration of the church in this specific sense also em-
phasise the privileges and responsibilities of membership of the local church, the discipline of its members
and their acceptance of the authority of their leaders
over them, and the need for present-day apostles to
ensure the well-being of the total church. They are
among those who urge fellow Christians to get out of
their denominations. Others of us intend to stay where
we are and work for the renewal of the church, in the
full meaning of the word, from within. That doesn't
mean that we deny the need for fully committed
membership, for purity of teaching and doctrine, and
for a proper biblical understanding of the authority and
responsibility of local church leadership. The desire is
the same; the strategy is different.

Where are people going? The spiritual ambition of the
restoration churches is very clear. They long to see the
Kingdom of God established in the world; this will come
about—they believe—through the work and witness of
the growing restoration churches. Such an ambition
and vision is a powerful challenge to the denominational
churches which often seem more inclined to settle for
maintenance and the status quo, rather than mission
and the ambition to grow.

In some ways the renewed denominational churches,
and the growing restoration churches are like the two
tracks of a railway line. Both are needed if the journey
is to be safely completed. The Lord longs that his
church shall be one; so both renewed churches and restoration churches should seek to draw closer together,
rather than pull apart or drift out of fellowship with
each other. It is good that the leaders meet together in

a number of ways, both nationally and locally. We need more of that.

We also need to ensure that those churches which are experiencing a measure of renewal don't stop short of all that God wants to do, but allow his Spirit to bring his new life not only to the members but also to the activities, purposes and structures of the church; that the renewal and restoration of the denominational churches is in accordance with New Testament patterns and principles. It is equally necessary that the life and witness of the restoration churches doesn't become dull, dry and formal. Their members also need the renewing breath of the Spirit.

Unlike the tracks of a railway line, the 'tracks' of restoration and renewal need to be as closely entwined as possible—with the purposes of Jesus, so that people are truly renewed and structures truly restored.

If you want more information, see 'Useful Books' on pages 152-154 for titles relating to this question.

Scripture teaches that we should care for the weaker brother. Shouldn't people with a renewal experience become more sensitive to the feelings of others?

Yes; but let's be clear about what Paul meant when he wrote about weaker brothers. In Romans chapter 14, he was addressing some social and cultural matters relating to personal behaviour, such as, in particular, eating meat that previously had been offered to idols in the heathen temples. He also referred to the attitude that some believers had about some days being more important than others. He wasn't addressing renewal issues. At the same time, he is stating a general principle about how Christians who disagree should behave towards one another; and this is relevant to our question which is really about how Christians with different spiritual experiences and personal and cultural backgrounds should relate to each other.

Those who have experienced renewal can, unwittingly, give the impression to other members of the congregation that they have arrived spiritually. There is the danger of spiritual pride and of people being hurt because the impression given, so often unintentionally, is that past spiritual teaching and experience has somehow been invalid and insufficient. And there may be those who have tasted renewal but then drawn back; these might find the freedom of those enjoying renewal even more distasteful.

Just as people experiencing renewal can hurt others in a congregation, so those who are ignorant of or actively resisting the renewing work of the Holy Spirit can also hurt, hold up and harm the fellowship of the local church. Pain and frustration can be experienced by different groupings in a church, and that brings the further danger of division over spiritual experience along the lines of the church at Corinth.

Of course, the tensions, divisions and emphases within a local church are also reflected in the wider Christian community both locally and nationally. Evangelicals on the reformed wing of the church can easily dismiss charismatics as a lunatic fringe; and those in renewal can judge their more traditional evangelical or Catholic brothers or sisters for 'quenching the Spirit'.

However, in the first place, the renewal of the church that God is concerned with may be much wider and deeper than just our view of charismatic, liturgical, catholic, or structural renewal. Secondly, whenever the gifts of the Holy Spirit—a key focus of renewal—are mentioned in the New Testament, it is always in the context of love within the fellowship. Look up Romans chapter 12, Ephesians chapter 4, 1 Corinthians chapters 12 to 14 and 1 Peter chapter 4 and check that out for yourself. Thirdly, our unity is not based upon our personal experience of renewal, but upon our personal commitment to Jesus as lord and head of the church, and we must ensure that each of us is holding fast to him. His headship is the key to solving so many of the troubles and tensions in our churches today.

But back to Romans chapter 14 where Paul reminds us of five essential principles that must operate in our fellowships where people differ.

● Differences of opinion—and experience—are not to hinder the fellowship (vs.3, 13, 15, 21).
● We are responsible and accountable to the Lord for our conduct. It should not hinder others. It must honour the Lord (vs.4, 6, 7, 10–12, 22).
● Each of us should be fully convinced in our own minds over what we do (vs.5, 23) and never do anything from prejudice or party spirit.
● Nothing is unclean in itself (vs.14, 20), and so all we offer in worship—whether informal worship, traditional canticle, structured prayer or a word of knowledge is acceptable to God when offered in spirit and truth.
● There are larger issues of righteousness and peace (vs.17–19) and—we might add—of the unity and mission of the church, to which we should be giving our thoughts.

Has the renewal movement caused churches or fellowships to focus more on personal testimony and sharing and less on serious Bible study?

This is an important question. It is often in this area of experience versus Bible study that critics of the renewal movement feel they have good cause for justified complaint. In many ways, the question can only invite a subjective response, because the situation will vary from church to church.

Three observations

First, the renewal movement has given individual Christians a greater experience of the Lord in their lives, and therefore a greater desire to witness to what God has done for them.

Secondly, strengthened by the Spirit, Christians are demonstrating a confidence in the Lord, and so are more ready and able to share what once they would have kept to themselves. Once people begin to share their testimony in this way, others are encouraged to do the same thing.

Thirdly, the renewing work of the Holy Spirit has clearly given us a greater thirst to know Christ and to want to know more of the Scriptures: witness the tremendous growth of Bible Weeks, Dales Weeks, Spring Harvest and all the events with a renewal label or flavour! What is different, it seems, is that people don't now come to the Bible just to grow in head knowledge; they come also to be strengthened in their life-changing relationship with God.

Three conclusions

It seems that many young Christians are rightly rejecting a dry, intellectual study of the Bible. They are not interested in truth unless it leads to life.

We need to note the danger that still exists of not opening the Bible at all in some 'renewed' circles. It is all singing, praise, testimony, and there is no feeding from the Scriptures. It is sadly true, too, that many people in the renewal movement have never been taught how to minister the true exposition of the Bible. There are dangers in both analytical and anecdotal approaches to the Bible; and it is all too possible to impose our experience upon its truths, rather than expound its truths to stimulate our experience.

This question reminds us that we need the right approach to the Word and the Spirit, in our personal Christian living, in the fellowship of our smaller groups and in the total life of our church. If we feed ourselves only on the Word of God, without the Spirit, we shall dry up. If we rely entirely upon the Spirit of God, without the Word, we shall blow up; but if we hold the truth of the Word and the power of the Spirit happily together, then we shall grow up.

I'm sure that it is the responsibility of each Christian and church to ask how they measure up in relation to the issues raised by this question. Over to you!

A Christian friend rejects the renewal movement, claiming it appeals more to the emotions than to the mind. How should I reply?

1 Peter 3:15 is a very good place to start: 'In your hearts set apart Christ as Lord. Always be prepared to give an answer to everyone who asks you to give the reason for the hope that you have. But do this with gentleness and respect, keeping a clear conscience.'

Peter lays down some very good general guidelines

for Christians who are called upon to defend their faith. Often, we can feel threatened by those who differ from us, we can polarise the issues, and we can categorise people. All these dangers will be avoided if we follow Peter's advice, and we shall find ourselves growing spiritually as well.

It may also be helpful to have some basic ground rules for situations such as the one suggested by the question.

Ground rules for good dialogue

● Listen to and watch your friends. We communicate by body language as well as words; while your friends may be saying one thing with their mouths, they may be telling you something far more important by the fact that they are (for example) restless and agitated—thus revealing that the issue may not be intellectual but emotional or experiential!

● Remember, therefore, that the problem they present you with may not be the main issue. Reasoning and excuses may be a smoke screen for something more important. We need to be aware of these things as we try to get to the heart of the matter.

● Watch yourself also. If you feel threatened and vulnerable or realise that your reply is inadequate, then your friends may have done you a good turn by making you examine yourself and your own faith.

● It is also good to make sure you are all talking about the same thing. You may feel, for example, that the topic under discussion is the renewal movement in all its breadth and power while your friends may be thinking of some weird experience of tongues or a rather feeble expression of prophecy. So clarify the issue.

Now for some specific answers to your question.

Emotions versus intellect

● The Bible regards us as whole people. 'We are here to love the Lord our God with all our heart, mind, strength and soul.' This includes our emotions. Often Christians have been frightened to express publicly and openly their emotions in their worship and relationship of Christ. However, mums have danced in praise of the Lord in the privacy of their kitchens, and men have poured out their souls to God in their personal prayer lives. James Dobson's book, *Emotions, Can You Trust Them?'* helpfully shows us how such emotions as guilt, love and anger can be rightly expressed in our lives.

● There are twin dangers we need to avoid. Some Christians exalt too highly the role of the mind, and almost institute reason as their final authority, while others seem almost anti-intellectual, and ask only, 'Does it work?' whereas the question, 'Is it true?' is also a good one. Leanne Payne, the distinguished American counsellor, has shown that our minds have an analytical function and also an intuitive aspect. Some people—perhaps men especially—only analyse topics and have no time for intuition. It may be impossible to understand some aspects of the renewal movement (e.g. tongues, a word of prophecy, or a picture) with the analytical part of our mental faculties. But it may be through intuition that others know whether or not the tongues or prophecy is of the Lord.

● Whatever our emotions and minds may be saying, we must stress that the truth about the renewal movement doesn't rest either on our understanding or on our experiences but on the truth of God's Word. In my own personal pilgrimage, I could not accept anything about the renewing work of the Spirit unless I knew that it was true in Scripture. I had to wrestle with such passages of the Bible as 1 Corinthians chapters 12 to 14 to sort out what they taught about the baptism of the Spirit and the gifts of the Spirit. I discovered that others were making the same journey and that God was moving in power in ways that I could not deny. My personal experience needed to catch up with my theology and biblical understanding. But first I had to be willing for God to break into my life and do a new thing over which I might not have much control; and at first I wasn't sure that I *was* willing.

● It is often just here—at the level of our will—that the real problem lies. I suspect that many readers have travelled a similar path to mine—unwilling for God to intervene until they reached a position of spiritual desperation and emptiness. Only then were they ready to come to the Lord on his terms and not theirs. Renewal, very simply, isn't a matter primarily of intellect or emotions; rather it is a matter of being spiritually dry and empty; of coming to the Lord Jesus and drinking from him; of discovering afresh the streams of living water flowing out from him through us to others all around. It is not something we should be arguing about; instead we should be praying that God in his mercy and grace will continue to renew his church and his people.

He is the Spirit of unity, but has renewal become more denominational?

Only God knows the full facts about the twentieth century renewal of his church in the power of his Spirit. But we can at least attempt some assessment of what is happening.

At first the renewal was mainly outside the denominational churches: members of those churches found leadership and encouragement through men like Canon Michael Harper, the invaluable work of the Fountain Trust and inspirational gatherings in cities and universities.

As people became stronger and more numerous, God led them to take the message and power back into their churches. At the same time, the house church movement grew. We began to see the setting up of organisations such as Anglican Renewal Ministries (ARM) and the Group for Evangelism and Renewal (GEAR) within the United Reformed Church. There were other groups within both the Protestant and Roman Catholic Churches as well as international groups such as the Sharing of Ministries Abroad (SOMA).

The fact is—God in his wisdom has been blessing the renewal in both the mainstream churches and the house churches. What really matters is that the Holy Spirit is a spirit of truth, prayer, holiness, mission and love and that we should expect the complete ministry and character of the Spirit of God to be fully manifested as the work of renewal continues, deepens and matures interdenominationally and internationally (or perhaps we should say *supra*-denominationally and *supra*-nationally).

Our church has been renewed in the Spirit for more than ten years, but the fire burns low today, as it does in my own heart. Have you any suggestions?

The letters to the seven churches and especially those to Ephesus and Sardis (Revelation 2:1 ff.; 3:1 ff.) suggest that this is not a new problem; and the good sales of Gordon MacDonald's book, *Restoring Your Spiritual Passion*, might indicate that many people today are aware of their spiritual poverty.

Sometimes it is helpful to understand why we may find ourselves in this state, before looking at possible remedies.

Possible causes of spiritual lowness

● You—and your church—may be carrying too great a weight of responsibility. You may be tackling man's agenda and not God's programme, and just wearing yourself out. Are you sure that all you are doing is what the Father wants you to do, or are you involved in what you feel you ought to be doing? Again, it is a matter of whether you are called by God or driven by men. It is good to check our activities against John 4:34.

● Satan will be at work to counteract the work of the Spirit, and he will especially use such weapons as discouragement, the fear of others and the temptation to compromise, to slow down or mark time in the work of renewal. It is good to check whether we have succumbed to any of these.

● Are there any areas of disobedience or unbelief before the Lord? These are two of the great road blocks that will prevent any further progress; and, since it is impossible to stand still in spiritual things, if we are not moving forward with God, then we are actually slipping backwards.

● Have you, possibly, come to a point where you have said to God that you are not prepared to move any further forward? Has he asked you to launch out into the depths of the Spirit whereas you prefer to play around in the shallow end?

● Stress or burn-out in the ministry may also be a factor.

They can bring physical and emotional exhaustion and will affect our spiritual vitality.

I wanted to survey those possible causes so that we would be able to understand the problem.

Some remedies
We are given some remedies for spiritual lowness in Leviticus 6: 8–13. Three times Moses is told that the fire must be kept burning—and that surely is the secret both for the church and yourself. Let me share six relevant thoughts from this passage:

● The fire must be kept burning (vs. 9, 12, 13). This was the Lord's command. This was what God expected. To be spiritually alive and on top ought to be the usual pattern of church-life, not something extra-special. So many of us live below the level that God expects. We are really made to feel out of step with others if we are in step with God. So don't let others discourage you or make you think that you are 'over the top'.
● It was the responsibility of the priest to make sure the fires were burning (v.9). The Old Testament priesthood has been replaced by the great high priesthood of Jesus and the priesthood of all believers. Thus our daily relationship with the Lord Jesus is crucial. The key to spiritual renewal is allowing Jesus to be lord day by day. He is the vine, we are the branches (John chapter 15). So many Christians fall down at this point. We replace our abiding in Jesus with frenzied activity, and wonder why things don't happen. The priest had to wear the right clothing (vs. 10–11) and this reminds us that as Christians we are to 'put off' attitudes and habits that deny our Christian witness and to 'put on' the Lord Jesus (you will see the details in Ephesians 4:17 ff.). Is there a

spiritual decline because we have the wrong spiritual clothing on?

● It was the burnt-offering (v.9) that was to be laid on the fire. The burnt offering was not the sacrifice for sin but the expression of joyful fellowship with the Lord. You will notice that the offering was to remain on the altar during the night as well as during the day. So it was to be a continual offering. This reminds us of our essential relationship with the Lord.

● Day by day the ashes of the fire were to be removed and taken right away (v.10). As Christians we are to remove all that would quench or grieve the work of the Holy Spirit. It is good to remind ourselves of the value of repentance in the Christian life: putting things right, making apologies and coming back to the Lord if we have wandered away; removing the unproductive parts in our lives. I wonder what the 'ashes' in your church or personal life would be. What's clogging up the work of the Spirit?

● With any fire, you not only remove the ashes. Every morning the priest had to add firewood (v.12) to stoke up the fires! Daily feeding of the fire is necessary. Sometimes we realise that we have neglected the 'wood' in our lives—we have slipped up on reading the Bible, gathering for fellowship, being constant in prayer or on other means of God's grace in our lives. Are you feeling spiritually cold because you haven't put any wood on the fire recently?

● Lastly, the priest had to burn the fat of the fellowship offering (v.12; see also Leviticus 7:12, 13, 15). This was the thank-offering; it reminds us of the vital part that thanksgiving and praise play in keeping the spiritual fires burning in our lives.

As we have seen, God had to tell Moses three times

to keep the fire burning. I'd like to suggest that you reflect quietly and slowly upon this short passage in the Old Testament so that the Spirit of God can speak very personally to you and your church. Which part of the detailed instruction do you personally need to respond to?

What is baptism of the Spirit?

This is one of the most controversial questions among evangelicals, charismatics and Pentecostals today! I hope that, as we attempt an answer, we can generate more light than heat, indicate some of the points of difference, and above all, help people into a much clearer understanding and experience of the Holy Spirit.

It is important that we bring our biblical understanding and our Christian experience together on this matter.

I believe there is a definite spiritual experience—sometimes called the baptism of the Spirit—taught in the New Testament (Matthew 3:11; Mark 1:8; Luke 3:16; John 1:33; Acts 1:5, 8; 11:15–17; 1 Corinthians 12:13). The Greek verb for baptise is either *bapto* or *baptizo*—meaning to dip or to drench. What is abundantly clear, especially from John 1:29, 33, is that the Lord Jesus exercises two ministries towards every individual: he bears away our sins as the Lamb of God and he is the one who will baptise us in the Spirit. It is clearly essential that we know both these ministries of Jesus, at a time when, sadly, some who have been baptised in water know neither of them! Every believer should—and can be—baptised in the Spirit. (Notice the words 'if any one' and 'all' in John 7:37–39; Acts 2:16–18, 38, 39.)

Every believer has the Holy Spirit–indeed you cannot be a true Christian unless you have been given the gift of the Holy Spirit. But not every believer is filled with the Holy Spirit. See, for example, Romans 8:9, Ephesians 5:18, 4:30 and 1 Thessalonians 5:19 where we are reminded of the need to be filled, and of the danger of grieving and quenching the Spirit. So the New Testament is making it plain that we can have the Holy Spirit, and know something of his work, ministry and presence, yet limit and restrict him in one way or another.

Also, every believer has been baptised or incorporated by the Spirit into the body of Christ (1 Corinthians 12:13). This is an important reference because Paul is saying to the church at Corinth that all of their members, whether they spoke in tongues or not, whether they had spectacular spiritual gifts or not, had been incorporated into the body of Christ. Often people seem to ignore the second part of the verse: 'and we were all given the one Spirit to drink'. Paul uses the same word for drink as Jesus did in John 7:37–39, when he was speaking about spiritual thirst and satisfaction.

What Paul was teaching, I believe, was that all believers are given, first, the awareness, once for all, that they belong to the fellowship of the body through the Spirit and, secondly, the spiritual capacity to receive more of the Spirit.

The area of controversy concerns baptism in the Spirit, ministered by Christ, to equip and empower his people for Christian service. The heart of the difficulty lies in whether such baptism is all part of our initial experience, or whether it is a very definite subsequent experience.

Perhaps I can best clarify this tension by referring to cures for colds! There are some capsules you can take which have the effect of releasing their healing powers at hourly intervals for up to twenty-four hours. You take the whole capsule, but the benefits are only received as a process. Others might take several tablets, one at a time, at four-hourly intervals. The second and subsequent taking of tablets is linked with the first, but each occasion is clearly separate and distinct.

The key verses are those in the Gospels and the Acts —which I quoted earlier. People have interpreted these in different ways. What is clear in the New Testament is that Jesus—at the very least—had both an initial and a subsequent experience of the Spirit in his ministry. He was born of the virgin Mary but conceived by the Holy Spirit. Before his baptism, he knew the ministry of the Holy Spirit, as witness his perfect wisdom and faultless holiness. But at his baptism, when he was equipped for his public ministry, he was endued with the fulness of the Spirit (see Luke 3:21ff.; 4:1; 14:17, 18).

The way many people seem to understand this matter is to see baptism into the body of Christ as being for salvation and the baptism of the Holy Spirit as being for service—the first giving us our position in Christ and the second equipping us with power.

We must be clear that the baptism of the Spirit is not the beginning of super-Christianity for some, though it should be the end of inferior-Christianity for all. It should be our introduction into the fulness of the Spirit; and, though baptised only once, we are commanded to go on allowing the Holy Spirit to fill us. To return to the cold cure tablets—I would equate the one initial filling with the tablet which is taken once but continues to release its power; and the many fillings with the tablets which need to be taken, one at a time, at certain intervals.

I personally find it helpful to teach what I believe is in

Scripture about this.

● There is the clear initial gift of the Holy Spirit, when I receive the Spirit and am sealed as belonging to Jesus (see Acts 2:38–39; Romans 8:9; 1 Corinthians 6:19; Ephesians 1:13).
● This may or may not be linked with a subsequent overwhelming by the Spirit, referred to as the baptism of the Spirit. Ideally the initiating into and the overwhelming by the Spirit are the same experience, but in practice this may not be so. Certainly the baptism of the Spirit is the gateway not the goal of Christian experience.
● There must be the constant filling by the Spirit (Ephesians 5:18). We need not only the initial baptism in the Spirit, but we need also to walk in the Spirit day by day (Galatians 5:16–25).

Another area of controversy is whether or not speaking in tongues is the essential sign to show that a person has been baptised in the Spirit. It would seem (from the Acts verses quoted above as well as Acts 2:4, 17; 8:14–17; 10:44–46; 19:6) that those who have been baptised in the Spirit may well find the gift of tongues has been given and released. We don't, however, believe the New Testament is teaching that such a gift *has* to be manifested—as the Pentecostals teach—to prove that a person has been baptised in the Spirit. Other more powerful evidence of this should include freedom and power in witness (Luke 24:48–49; Acts 1:8); the fruit of the Spirit, as we respond to the command to be filled with the Spirit (Galatians 5:22–23; Ephesians 5:18); the release of the gifts of the Spirit, as the believer acknowledges and submits to the lordship of Jesus.

The baptism of the Spirit is not the peak of spiritual experience for a few super-Christians; rather (I believe)

it is the normal spiritual provision that Jesus has planned
and provided for each one of his children.

How can I be sure that I have been baptised in the Spirit?

I take it that the questioner is asking about an initial
filling of the Holy Spirit.

There are three grounds on which we can be sure that
we have experienced this.

First, the Word of God promises us that Jesus will
baptise us in the Spirit (see John 1:33; 7:37; Acts 1:4, 5,
8; 2:4ff.). If we have fulfilled the conditions set out in
the Bible—turning from known sin, seeking to be obedient, longing to be baptised in the Spirit and to glorify
Jesus—then we must trust the promise of the Bible and
not allow Satan to sow seeds of doubt; he often does
this when Christians, having asked for the baptism of
the Spirit, find that nothing seems to happen.

Secondly, you will begin to find the Holy Spirit making
his presence felt within your life. People have described
the effects of this. Some have spoken of a fountain deep
within, bursting out; or of the Bible as being no longer
like a black-and-white television picture but like a full-
colour one; or of temptations being broken; or of a new
and deep awareness of Jesus; or of the release of power
or the coming of a deep peace; or of the realisation for
the first time that God is their Father.

Thirdly, some external changes and signs may come.
Some Christians have been temporarily paralysed by
the Spirit, unable to move; others just 'rest in the Spirit';
others find they have the gift of tongues released; for
others this gift is released days or even years later.

People will be aware of a new love and peace in their life. The self-confident person may be 'knocked down' by the Spirit; the fearful becomes gentle; the pessimist experiences a 'high'; the withdrawn becomes an outgoing person.

While the Spirit's work and ministry is the same, the way he comes upon people will vary greatly. Don't try to copy a particular experience. You don't even need to ask another Christian to pray for you and lay hands on you; you can know the baptism in the solitude of your own room. On the other hand, some people have found it a great help to ask another Christian to pray for them to know the baptism of the Spirit.

Our experience may be governed by the hang-ups and baggage that we all bring—past hurts, fears, assumptions. What the Lord looks for is not some special technique of laying on of hands, but the genuine longing of hungry and thirsty hearts to know more of Christ. When the heart is right, we shall know the baptism of the Spirit—and we shall not be able to keep it to ourselves, whether we want to or not!

When I was first baptised in the Holy Spirit, the Lord seemed very close and I regularly heard him speaking to me. Now, for no obvious reason, he no longer seems so near. Is this normal?

Whether it is normal or not, many people have similar experiences.

I would like to say, first of all, that it is important to distinguish between our feelings, on the one hand, and what the Scriptures promise us, on the other.

The awareness and joy of the Lord's presence is

something very precious; it may stand in marked contrast to a person's experience before he was baptised in the Spirit. It can feel like being in love. There is a danger of resting in such a past experience rather than in a present relationship with Jesus; of putting the experience before the Lord himself.

In a lovely picture in Isaiah 50:4–5, the Lord is described as waking us morning by morning and speaking to us personally; and Jesus spoke about our being his friends and about his sharing his mind and purpose with us as we obey his commands (John 15:14–15).

We are not only to rejoice in our newly-discovered relationship with Jesus, but also, daily, to abide in him (John chapter 15); this happens as we *daily* allow him to cleanse us from any sin (vs.2–3), express our utter dependence upon him (v.4), read the Scriptures and allow his word to dwell in our hearts (v.7) and yield ourselves afresh to his purposes (v.10).

As we do those things, our relationship and experience of the Lord's presence and power will become brighter and brighter again (see Proverbs 4:18).

Some members of my church speak of being filled with the Spirit. What do they mean?

Being filled with the Spirit has always been part of the normal Christian life. The Acts of the Apostles records both groups and individual people who were filled with the Spirit (see Acts chapter 2:4; 4:8; 6:3; 11:24) and Paul, writing to the church at Ephesus, commands them to be filled with the Spirit (Ephesians 5:19). The actual words that Paul uses mean, 'All of you are to allow the Holy Spirit to go on filling you.' Thus the fulness of the Spirit was to be the mark of the normal Christian life, rather than the sign of extraordinary Christian living.

Being filled with the Spirit and being drunk are experiences which affect people's behaviour. The people themselves may not be aware that this is so but others all around certainly will be!

The purpose of the Spirit is to glorify Jesus (John 16:13, 14); to produce the characteristics or fruit of the Spirit, such as peace, love, joy (Galatians 5:22, 23); to display the gifts or ministries of the Spirit (1 Corinthians 12:7–11); and to promote holiness in Christian living (Romans 8:5ff.) and praise in worship (Ephesians 5:19–20). As a person is filled with the Spirit, he will show more and more evidence of the presence and ministries of the Spirit in his life.

Although each Christian has the gift of the Spirit (Acts 2:38; Romans 8:9), all Christians need to allow the Lord Jesus to baptise them in the Spirit (John 1:33) —to give them an initial filling of the Spirit—and then to allow the Spirit to go on filling them.

There are conditions to be fulfilled and various practical steps we can take if we want this to happen. We may need to repent of some sin or disobedience (Acts 3:19); we shall certainly want to make sure that there are no areas in our lives where we are disobeying the Lord Jesus (Acts 5:32); we must desire to be filled with the Spirit and thirsty for all that God wants to give us (John 3:37–39); and then we ask the Lord to go on giving his Spirit to us (Luke 11:13), trusting him to keep his promises to his children (Galatians 3:1–5).

A final word: some Christians are frightened of the Holy Spirit. But the New Testament clearly says that the Holy Spirit is not a Spirit of fear (Romans 8:15; 2 Timothy 1:6–7). So we can give the Lord Jesus any fears and worries we may have and ask him to give us a fresh filling of the Spirit so that we may glorify him in our daily living.

I am worried about grieving or quenching the Holy Spirit. Is this the same as the sin against the Holy Spirit which Jesus says cannot be forgiven?

It is possible to grieve or quench the Spirit because he is a person (the third person of the Trinity); but I don't believe that grieving or quenching the Spirit is the same thing as committing the unforgivable sin. Let's look at the contexts in which these things are referred to.

The reference to grieving the Spirit (Ephesians 4:30) is in the context of teaching about our practical daily living—our work and speech, our reactions and emotions. As Christians indwelt by the Spirit we can grieve him if we respond to the flesh and not to the Spirit.

The reference to quenching the Spirit (1 Thessalonians 5:19) is in the context of Paul's instructions to the Thessalonian Christians about the right use of spiritual gifts in the church. They were not to put out the Spirit's fire; they were not to treat prophecies with contempt—rather they were to test everything to discern what God had given; and they were to hold to the good and avoid the evil.

The sin against the Holy Spirit (Matthew 12:32; Mark 3:29) is mentioned in the account of a dispute Jesus had with the Pharisees. They were accusing him of demon expulsion by means other than the Holy Spirit. They were deliberately rejecting the evidence of the Holy Spirit at work, and trying to explain what was happening in other ways. So long as they were doing this, repentance and forgiveness were, by definition, not possible.

The best way of ensuring that we don't quench or grieve the Spirit is by allowing him to go on filling and changing us.

2

The Local Church

What are the important questions when selecting a local church?

This is a question of our time, for the first Christians would have joined themselves to—or been added to—the local church. It's the sort of question that might be asked by people moving to a new area and wanting to sort out churches before buying a house; or by new—or young—Christians wanting to find a church for the first time; or by people considering whether they should commute to some famous, well-attended city centre church or join the local church round the corner. Whatever the reasons, the important questions to ask about a church are:

● Is it a church where Christ is lord and head or are there personalities and factions controlling it?
● Is it a church where you will receive fresh spiritual bread from the Bible or stale crusts from other sources?
● Is it a church where the Holy Spirit is free to work as he wishes, or is he safely controlled? (You can often get a good idea of what the church 'officially' teaches about the Holy Spirit by looking at the bookstall.)

• Is it a church which is outward-looking in evangelism towards the parish and area, and with a missionary heart towards the world, or is it dull, inward-looking and showing signs of 'fellowshipitis'?

• Is it a church where you will soon be able to find your place to serve the Lord or will you have to be there for ten years before you are accepted by the locals?

• Is it a church where you and other members of the family will feel socially and personally at home and comfortable—a place to which you are proud to belong —or does the whole set-up embarrass you?

• If you are a Christian whose Monday–Friday/Saturday work and calling means you are constantly giving out to others, is it a place where you will be supported and encouraged or will many church members be frightened of your membership?

• Are there any emphases in worship, doctrine or practice with which you will be uncomfortable?

• Is it a church that cares for people and displays the love of the Lord?

• Is it the church—because of the above, or even in spite of some of the answers to the above questions—to which you know the Lord is leading you, and about which you have the Lord's peace?

These are ten important and searching questions. No church is perfect, and we all fall short in many ways, but answering these questions might help you to recognise the sort of church you should be looking for, and which existing church members should be working towards becoming.

For more than ten years my parish church has held healing services, encouraged us to seek spiritual gifts, and sung renewal choruses. There has been no division but steady growth. Our new vicar, however, in many ways a fine man, has stopped the healing services and made known his opposition to anything charismatic. I have hesitated to join the thirty or so who have left to join the local community church but am grieved at his repeated attempts to hinder the Spirit. What should I do?

This is a hot potato, and there are no easy answers! But there are some important considerations.

You say the new vicar has stopped the healing services, and is opposed to things charismatic, but I wonder whether you know why. Just as a couple come to their wedding with hopes for the future and the fears, hurts and baggage of the past, so a Christian minister brings to a new church his past experience, understanding and hurts. Is the opposition based on different understanding of the biblical teaching or does it have its root cause at a much deeper personal and experiential level?

The qualities any minister values in his congregation are their love and support. Your new vicar will appreciate your support and your prayers for him and with him. Such fellowship will be a very powerful and healing force.

Equally, you have every right to expect that your vicar should lead the whole church forward as the Holy Spirit leads and as the head of the church, the Lord Jesus Christ, directs. There are rights and responsibilities on both sides (Hebrews 13:7, 17). Previously you and other church members have received and used spiritual gifts. It is important that you should continue to use them; for one thing, gifts not used will atrophy and die. Can you use your gifts in house groups and in individual ministry? Remember that while you are to submit to those over you in the Lord, you are also to submit to the Lord himself, and that if there is a conflict of loyalties, you must obey God (Acts 4:19–20).

You are obviously considering very prayerfully whether it would be right to leave your present church. The Bible teaches that we must withstand and separate from those who deny the truth of Jesus as the Son of God, or who twist the nature of the gospel and justification by faith (Galatians chapters 1, 2; 1 John 4:1–3). But there are many other issues—such as church order, other doctrines, forms and content of worship, and clashes of personalities—which do not provide grounds for leaving. Paul urges us (Ephesians 4:3, 13) to make every effort to keep the unity of the Spirit in the bond of peace until we all reach the unity of the faith.

We believe that you should only leave the church if you feel you have no other course of action, and if you have the peace and permission of the Lord about it. A number of Christians facing the same situation as yourself have found great fellowship and blessing in joining the equivalent to the local community church you mention, and God is using the house church movement in a remarkable way. Have you, however, explored the possibilities of there being another church of your own denomination where you would be equally at home? That would save you changing both your fellowship and your denomination.

How can different traditions and styles of worship and music mix and blend?

This is one of those questions more and more people are facing in our local churches.

In some ways worship can be likened to marriage. Do you sometimes wonder how two seemingly very different people manage to hit it off in their marriage? Similarly, people wonder how the singing of a canticle and a simple worship song can be combined in the same service. The secret lies in understanding three things.

The principle of oneness must underlie marriage and should underlie our worship. Whatever our own experience, personality, culture and preference, we should each be able to confess that Jesus is our saviour and lord, and that the Holy Spirit has made us one in him. Our unity is found in Christ, even though we may be expressing it in different forms of worship.

In good marriages, husbands and wives, though very different in character and personality, have their own roles to play and need their own space: one partner does not dominate the other. It should be like that in worship. One form, tradition or style of worship and music should not dominate the others. All should be mutually enriching. Christians, however different, should come to appreciate one another increasingly, just as partners in a good marriage do.

Different personalities in a marriage take time, in practice, to establish firm bridges between one another's lives, as well as understanding, patience, love and communication. The same is true with worship. We need to work at bridging from one style to another. We should take time explaining the changes we want to introduce.

We can show that freedom and form in worship—the

spirit and the structure—are not in opposition, but can provide a beautiful harmony that will increasingly edify the church and bring glory and joy to God.

It has been suggested that in the name of Christ we can pronounce the forgiveness of sins to another Christian. Is this a neglected or a dangerous doctrine?

In various places (e.g. Matthew 6:14–15; John 20:23; Ephesians 4:32; James 5:14–16) we are taught to forgive one another. Two different words are used in the Greek. One means to lift a burden from another person and take it away completely. The second means to bestow a favour unconditionally on them. Such forgiveness is found only in the finished work of Jesus and in his name (see Mark 2:7; 1 John 1:9; Ephesians 1:7). Only Jesus can ultimately lift the burden and bestow the blessing.

Sin, however, doesn't affect just God. It has its personal and social implications; and I believe that we need to ask for and assure others of forgiveness much more often than we do. Much inner healing is needed today because there is unconfessed and unforgiven sin in many lives. We don't always find it easy in a Christian fellowship to expose our weaknesses, needs and failings. Instead, we hide behind masks for fear of being judged and rejected. But there is a great need for us to be willing to be vulnerable before one another, to confess our sins to each other and to forgive one another.

In *The Father Heart of God* Floyd McClung has written: 'A good rule of thumb to follow is, if it is a secret sin, confess it to God; if it is a private sin, ask forgiveness of the one you have sinned against; and if it is a public sin, ask the group's forgiveness.'

I would like to add that we need to make the distinction between the sin that needs to be forgiven, the wound that needs to be healed and the bondage from which we need to be set free.

One other point: the church orders its life so that its ministers are authorised officially and publicly to pronounce to the people that God forgives their sins. Other members of the body must not take to themselves that which they are not authorised to do. However, all of us, I believe, are instructed in the Scriptures to assure people, often in a counselling situation, that God has forgiven them—and (where appropriate) that we have forgiven them also.

Is there a case for suspending from the Lord's Table, until he or she shows genuine repentance, someone whose sin has brought discredit on the church?

This is a question about church discipline. On the whole, the church and her authorities have side-stepped such issues and have tolerated sexual immorality and doctrinal error among members and ministers for too long in this country and other parts of the world.

There is quite a bit about discipline in the New Testament. See what happened, for example, in the case of the woman taken in adultery (John 8:1–11); of the dishonesty of Ananias and Sapphira (Acts chapter 5); of incest at Corinth (1 Corinthians 5:1–5); and remember the general principle that the Lord disciplines those whom he loves (Hebrews 12:6).

There are two dangers to avoid. The first is to act in a way which suggests that sin doesn't matter. Although

Christ has died and sin can be forgiven, we still need to
state that sin is an offence to ourselves, others and,
especially, God himself, who is holy. Discipline in the
church—for example, counselling a person not to come
to the Lord's Table for a period of time (as I have
personally done)—will demonstrate to the church both
the seriousness of sin and the reality of a person's
shame and repentance. The other danger is to focus on
certain sins—especially sexual and matrimonial, thus
giving the impression that adultery is more serious than
stealing or gossiping (see James 2:9–13). All sin, in
breaking God's law, is an offence to God's nature.

There are also two issues to note. First, greater
accountability arises from greater responsibility within
the church. In the pastoral epistles—see 1 Timothy
chapter 3—higher moral standards are expected from
those in positions of leadership. The same was true for
Timothy himself (1 Timothy 4:12) who had to set the
believers an example (see also Hebrews 13:7,17).
Secondly, the Lord's Table is both the occasion of deep
fellowship and the demonstration of the saving love of
Jesus; therefore it needs to be held in honour and respect—hence the instructions given in 1 Corinthians
5:9–13; 11:27–32.

Finally, there are two motives to safeguard. First, all
discipline in the New Testament is to be positive—
maintaining the holiness of the Lord and the welfare of
the person being disciplined. God acts out of love towards us, and we must do the same towards others.
Secondly, we need to remember that it is only those
without sin who cast the first stone. Or, as both Jesus
and Paul put it, in judging others we must be doubly
sure that we are not guilty of some different sin ourselves (see Matthew 7:1–5; Romans 2:17–24).

Some of us face the danger of compromise, others of

condemnation. The right biblical balance on this issue of discipline is to act out of love for fellow-Christians, a desire to uphold the honour of the Lord, and obedience to the leading of the Spirit. In that way, we won't go far wrong in tackling these very important but sensitive issues.

You might like to read Donald Bridges book about church discipline: *Spare the Rod and Spoil the Church* (MARC Europe).

No one, simply no one, ever preaches in our church except the ordained clergy. Should I talk to my vicar about it?

There may be a number of hidden issues in the question. Congregations can and do get frustrated if the members feel they could do the task of preaching, or leading or chairing a meeting, better than the appointed person. But the vicar or minister may feel guilty about delegating what he or others may feel he has been paid to do, to someone who has his own full-time job. Also, we clergy can feel very threatened by people who seem more capable than we are of doing 'our job'!

As well as the hidden agenda within this question, there are also some very important principles to disentangle.

● *The role of the clergy*. Some churches have reached a stage where the lay people believe anything the clergy can do, they can do better. The logical conclusion is, 'Why do we need a paid ministry?' Read again Ephesians 4:12 where Paul teaches us about the ministry gifts of apostle, prophet, teacher, pastor and evangelist—whose full-time task is to equip the saints for the work of ministry. So there is a God-appointed task for the minister to do; and there are tasks the minister has *not* been called to do; and everyone in the church needs to agree about this. Maybe the vicar is having to do tasks he is not ordained to do and which, if he could delegate to others, would set him free to spend more time in prayer and preparation for his preaching.

● *The expectations of the people.* Sometimes the hopes and expectations of the people are in line with the teaching of the Bible. On other occasions, they need to be challenged, taught and reformed according to the Word of God. Where there is a real difference between expectations and realisation, there will be stress and strain in the vicar. Clearly the New Testament teaches us that we have to be willing to relinquish those tasks that are not God-given, in order to concentrate upon the ones that are.

● *The discernment and use of gifts.* Obviously there must be occasions within a local church where people have the opportunity to develop their teaching and preaching gifts—in the sharing of a testimony, for example, in a smaller congregation or fellowship group or as part of a team visiting another parish. The Anglican church isn't geared to encouraging lay people to develop their gifts; so, if we want this to happen, we will need to make room for Spirit to work in this matter. (See also pages 84 to 86.)

● *The value of lay preaching.* There will obviously be special occasions when a particular theme or situation would be better handled by a specialist from within the congregation—for example, a doctor, social worker or economist—and there will also be times when missionaries home on leave could preach. There is value in asking lay people to share their faith and experience about prayer, temptation, the growth of faith—not least because others may well be able to identify with them—ordinary people like themselves—rather than with the clergy.

● *The need to support and encourage.* Don't forget that all of us bloom under the sunshine of opportunity and encouragement.

I'd like to ask some direct questions. How often do members of the congregation encourage with favourable comments the minister after he has preached? Does your vicar get extra time for a regular reading week? Is he encouraged to attend some relevant conference or 'in-service' training? (Those who are constantly giving out need to be able to take in, otherwise they will become dull and predictable, worn out and burnt out.) What financial help is your leader given to buy books to keep his reading up to date? Do a group of praying members—or leaders—meet before the service to pray for the Lord's blessing on all that is going to happen, to minister to the minister and to be open to anything the Lord would share before the worship begins? (Since we have been doing that—among other things—we have seen the evening congregation virtually double itself.)

If you have thought through all the above, then I think you should pray about the situation and be ready to talk to your vicar about it, when God gives you the right occasion.

My friend who was baptised as an infant has recently come to Christ and now has a strong compulsion to be baptised by immersion. The vicar has said don't. Help!

This is a problem I have often faced in the ministry as have many other Christians and their ministers. I would like to open up four aspects of this issue: the need of the individual Christian; the conviction of the minister; the solution in this instance; the pastoral way forward in the future.

The desire to be baptised by immersion as an adult can spring from uncertainty as to whether the person should have been baptised as an infant at all. (Was at least one of their parents a committed Christian?) It can also arise from a persistent inner conviction from the Spirit and the wish to be obedient to God, in being baptised in a way that seems to harmonise more exactly to the teaching and meaning of the New Testament—especially Romans chapter 6. So we must not, I believe, ignore or belittle such requests from newly converted Christians.

The minister knows that baptism is the sacrament ordained of God. As an Anglican, he believes that there are two groups of people who have the right to be baptised—the children of Christian parents (or at least of one Christian parent), and adults upon the confession of faith. He also believes that baptism is the outward sign and seal of the inward work of God's regenerating Spirit and cannot be repeated. He may well long to have a baptistry in his own church so that he can personally baptise adults by immersion. He might also have his suspicions as to whether some children whom he baptises *should* be baptised—not being as sure as he would wish to be about the Christian faith and commitment of their parents—but he doesn't believe he has the right to stand in judgement on their understanding and faith: that is God's prerogative. So when he says, 'Don't be re-baptised,' he is acting in accordance with his own conscience and convictions—as well as in obedience to church order and discipline. I hope that church members will appreciate his position.

I assume that the friend and the vicar have met and talked the issues through together. It is essential both that the friend should understand what the vicar is saying about baptism and its meaning, and that the minister should appreciate the spiritual compulsion in the heart of the new Christian.

There are some alternative possibilities they could explore. The new Christian could give her testimony and be publicly prayed for. Perhaps, alternatively or as well, her baptismal vows, made when a baby, could be reaffirmed in some way. If at the end of the day she still feels it is right to be baptised by immersion, then we clergy must not quench the Spirit. I believe we should explain that though we cannot be personally involved, we will pray for those who want to be baptised again, support them and do all we can to prevent them feeling they are 'playing spiritual truant'. They are still members of the church family, and our spiritual responsibility.

This problem will not go away, however much we may wish it would! The way forward must involve asking searching questions.

How effective are our infant baptism policy and procedures? Do we, as often as we ought, teach the full meaning of baptism or demonstrate publicly its joy and solemnity? Are we grasping this nettle in the Church of England? While taking our stand firmly upon the 'oneness' of baptism, do we need to introduce a recognised rite for the reaffirming of baptismal vows involving immersion and its symbolism of dying to sin and rising to new life in Christ? Is it possible to stress that this is *not* a re-baptism—we are not denying God's work—but a reaffirmation of our commitment to him as an adult?

How can I introduce the renewing work of the Spirit into my church?

There are usually three groups of Christians who ask this frequently-posed question. First, there are Christians who have very recently come to an experience of renewal themselves, are thrilled with what they know of the Lord and long that others should enter into the same experience of his Spirit.

The second group are Christian leaders who are moving to new churches and fellowships. They have moved from a church moving in renewal to one which is not.

The third group are either those ministers in renewal who are finding their hopes and plans blocked by fearful and frustrating members of their congregations, or church members in renewal who find that their clergy and church leaders don't want to have anything to do with things charismatic—perhaps because the church down the road was split by the renewal movement, and they are not going to have that happen in their church!

I believe the same answer applies to all three groups, although its outworking will depend on the circumstances and personalities concerned and, above all, on how the Lord leads.

First, renewal is God's work and not ours. I hope this book makes that clear. We are called to make way for the Spirit. According to our definition of renewal, it is clearly God's work by the Spirit. So it will be God who introduces it and brings it about in churches and fellowships. What is exciting is to discover that the tide of God's Spirit is coming in and won't be blocked for ever by our cold and stubborn hearts. So take courage and keep hoping!

Secondly, God seems to use people as his agents in bringing renewal to others and there are three responses we can make, whatever our circumstances—whether they encourage or discourage us.

We can pray and seek the Lord, and wait for his Spirit to come. Isn't this what Ezekiel did in his vision (chapter 37)? Weren't the apostles told to ask the Father to give them the Holy Spirit (Luke 11:13)? So, surely, this is where we start.

We can teach about the person and work of the Spirit. Surely we are called to pass on what the Bible is teaching us about the work of the Spirit. We don't only have to teach from the pulpit. Some of you will be in situations where doing that would be plainly impossible. But we can teach and share through books, tapes and simple personal testimony.

Some of you will be in a position to invite a small team from another church and fellowship to share what has happened in their church. Thus teaching and powerful testimony can be combined. What might not be well received from the home team can sometimes be acceptable from visitors, even if it leaves you feeling, 'That's exactly the same as I have been telling our folks for the last six months!' Don't give up! Didn't even Jesus experience the fact that a prophet is without honour in his home town?

Be patient and be bold. Be sensitive to know when the Holy Spirit is calling you to wait on his timing and opportunity, on the one hand, and yet be bold to grasp with faith the opportunities that God will give you, on the other. Whitsun and Pentecost provide natural

opportunities for introducing the renewing work of the
Spirit and certain contexts might be more conducive
than others: a series of talks and sermons about the
work of the Spirit; people sharing about renewal within
small fellowship groups or at a larger celebration of
several churches; a houseparty, particularly if people
have gone there feeling that they have got stuck and
wanting to move forward.

May I share two promises that are very precious to
me? Psalm 114:8 speaks of God who 'turned the rock
into a pool, the hard rock into springs of water'. That is
what God has done for us, although I had wondered, a
few years before, what could possibly move rock that
seemed so hard. So why can't the Lord turn your hard
situation into the pools and springs of renewal? The
second promise I am claiming for a very special situation, but I'd still like to share the verses with you:
'Forget the former things; do not dwell on the past.
See, I am doing a new thing! Now it springs up, do you
not perceive it? I am making a way in the desert and
streams in the wastelands. For I will pour water on the
thirsty land and streams on the dry ground; I will pour
out my Spirit on your offspring, and my blessing on
your descendants. They will spring up like grass in a
meadow, like poplar trees by flowing streams. One
will say, "I belong to the Lord"; another will call himself by the name of Jacob; still another will write on his
hand, "The Lord's", and will take the name Israel'
(Isaiah 43:18–19; 44:3–5).

Why don't you begin to ask the Lord to give you a
particular promise from the Bible about your situation?
Then, having received it, take it daily to the Lord in
prayer, asking him to fulfil it in his way and in his time?
I am sure you will be in for some lovely surprises!

Many feel that renewal means doing away with liturgy and set services. I know that this is only half the story. Can you help me to be clear about this?

This is such a vital topic. Worship affects us all. It can become divisive or draw the church closer together. Whether worship gives us pain or pleasure will be governed by a number of important considerations.

First, there are *false assumptions* that people often bring to worship. For example, some people believe that freedom of worship comes simply by abandoning the liturgy. This is not necessarily so. People who do abandon one form of liturgy sometimes end up by imposing another. Unstructured worship can become as repetitive in its own way as structured worship. We must beware, too, of thinking that renewal necessitates the rejection of all that is familiar and loved by thousands of worshippers.

Another assumption is that structure is unimportant or even unnecessary. But it is needed, just as a fire that is to be under control and useful needs a fireplace. Freedom in a framework is what most people find to be the best. Surely the principles of John 4:24 and 1 Corinthians 14:40 are to be held together!

There is also the false assumption that the Spirit is unable to guide what is planned in advance—whether it is preaching a sermon or singing an anthem.

Secondly, abandoning false assumptions, we must develop *biblical attitudes* to worship. For many people, worship is a matter of singing hymns and saying prayers for an hour or so on a Sunday. What a travesty of the truth! Worship is fundamentally the relationship of people with God, and God with people. Our heart and mind meet with the heart and mind of God himself. Thus, we shall find that our worship grows and changes.

We shall also find, in corporate worship, that people are at very different stages of spiritual growth—some will find a form of worship just what they need, for others it might be lightweight or too heavy.

Since worship is primarily a spiritual relationship, it is essential that both parties have the opportunity to express themselves. Many believe we should be giving space for this to happen within the framework of a liturgy. Christians who have experienced the renewal of the Spirit long to have space to worship God in some of the beautiful worship songs that have been written and may also find it most edifying to sing in the Spirit as well as with the mind. On the other hand, we need to give space for God to speak, and moving quickly from one part of the liturgy to another is not likely to be conducive to this.

We have found it a great help to have a time of worship followed by periods of silence during which there may be words of prophecy or knowledge or God may just meet with and minister to us individually as we are quiet before him. At first, many of us found the silence threatening but we have now grown to find it most helpful.

Thirdly, there needs to be care and sensitivity in the *practical action* we take. Some ministers and clergy may be anxious about making any changes at all but others —including Anglicans—feel free to ring the changes within the framework of the liturgy. The Bible tells us that the letter kills, but the Spirit gives life—which surely must be our guideline. What we have to be clear about is that we don't mistake the Spirit's guidance for the vicar's preference!

Among the gifts of the Spirit listed in 1 Corinthians chapter 12 is the gift of administration. A chairman shows this gift when he steers people through an agenda—rather as a helmsman might steer a boat through the water. There is a great need today for sensitive steering of our worship. This involves explaining the meaning of anything new that happens within a service and, if appropriate, the reasons for any changes.

We shall need to keep our standards high, and our worship as rich as possible using all the available resources there are. We must not fall into the trap of rejecting all that is old, and producing a generation of Christians who are ignorant of the great hymns of the past, and nourished only on the milk of lightweight spiritual experience.

The key issue is not about changing the furniture of the liturgy around to suit the latest whim, but about changing the hearts of the worshippers—and that is the work of the Spirit.

Can you give me some guidelines to make it easier to introduce changes into our church?

The fact of change in the churches is here to stay. Change is a feature of life. We may have to battle over changing a hymn tune, or a hymn book, but hymns themselves were new-fangled things in the nineteenth century.

The renewal movement is bringing about many changes—from styles of leadership and the content of our worship services, to the architecture and furnishing of our churches. Change, handled in the right way, can be considerably less traumatic than change brought about in an insensitive manner.

Some principles in a time of change
● Explain simply and clearly what the changes are, and

why the changes are being introduced. Explain *before* rather than *after* the changes occur.

● Involve others in the process of change. We have no right, I believe, to impose changes over the heads of our church members. We need to involve them in a simple process of consultation—letting them express their views, thoughts and fears. We would be wise to involve others in the church in the actual decisions about change, so that the responsibility is a corporate and not an individual one.

● Give people time to assimilate the change into their thinking. We can so easily forget that problems and hopes which we have wrestled with in our minds for six months can't be taken on board and accepted by others in six minutes. Give others time to understand and to test and accept your thinking.

● Be certain of God's timing and will in the change.

● Give opportunity to people who are hurting and fearful about the proposed changes to express those fears and hurts. As we are open with each other, we shall discover whether people are reacting because they have misunderstood what is proposed; whether they are fearful about how the change will affect them; whether they have no confidence in what is proposed; whether they are worried about any financial implications or consider—from their professional knowledge—that the plans have been poorly researched or presented; or whether they are just opposed to change of any sort!

● Make use of experimental periods—of, say, three to six months. Try things out, if the proposed changes can be introduced in this way. Change doesn't seem so final brought about this way. At the same time things can be tested, refined, altered if wrong, and welcomed when they are seen to be right.

● Avoid using emotive language when talking about

change. We need to be sensitive to one another's hopes and fears, vulnerabilities and hurts. A time of change should surely be a time when the fellowship focuses on the love and purpose of the Lord and avoids rubbing each other up the wrong way or confronting one another.

The process of change

It's important to understand the process of change. According to Dr Roy Pointer of the Bible Society there are four stages in that process.

- Knowledge—the 'what' and the 'why' of change.
- Persuasion—explaining in personal terms what positive benefits will come to us as a result of these changes.
- Decision—to go ahead with the change.
- Confirmation—as the church looks back in six to twelve months' time, realises that the changes have been right and confirms the decisions.

The price of change

Sometimes change is introduced happily. Often there is a price to pay when change is mooted. A group of church leaders from larger churches were discussing what aspects of their church life they found most difficult to face. Without exception, everyone in the group confessed it was facing the cost that comes when change is in the air. There is often an emotional cost, demands are made upon the family, and periods of stress and pain have to be faced. I personally found it helpful to realise that the one who brought about the greatest change was Jesus. He faced the cost of change in his ministry. He challenged Jewish legalism and religion in order to introduce God's way of salvation through grace and faith. At the heart of our faith is the price of change—the cross. Any change and subsequent cost we face will be very small in comparison with that which Jesus faced.

As you understand the process of change, put into practice the principles for change, and find inspiration in Jesus who faced the price of change, it will be easier to bring about change in your church as the Lord leads you.

Do apostles exist today?

Christians in the house church movement would answer, 'Yes,' Roman Catholic believers might query whether we were talking about bishops in the apostolic succession—and the rest of us would be puzzled, or say we don't know—although we belong to the one, holy, catholic and apostolic church! Before coming to an answer, let's look at the evidence.

The meaning of apostle

Simply, apostle means a sent one, and apostleship—a sending forth. However, it is right to speak of three categories of apostle:

● The unique apostleship of Jesus, who was sent by the Father (Hebrews 3:1). Often Jesus is described as 'the sent one' in John's Gospel.
● The specific group of the twelve apostles who were called and sent out by the Son (Revelation 21:14). The unrepeatable nature of their ministry lay in the fact that they were eye-witnesses of Jesus, and the resurrection. Some of them fulfilled the ministry of writing parts of the New Testament under the inspiration of the Spirit

and, with the prophets, they were the foundation stones, the pillars or the hall-mark of the church (Ephesians 2:20; 3:5).

● The unlimited and continuing group of apostles who were sent out by the Spirit. (Note the role of the Trinity in a full understanding of apostleship.) Such people as Barnabas, James, Junias and Silas were called apostles (Acts 14:4; Galatians 1:19; Romans 16:7; 1 Thessalonians 2:6). So the word apostle was given to those men and possibly women?—who had either a unique or a broadly-based role.

The ministry of the apostle
The evidence of the New Testament teaches us that the apostles had a three-fold ministry in relation to:

● *The message of the gospel.* The ministry of an apostle was to do with the good news, revealed to and written down by the apostles, which was to be the foundation of the church. The apostles were to teach and pass on to others the message of the gospel.

● *The mission of the church.* It is clear from the Acts of the Apostles that the apostles were usually the spiritual trail-blazers, breaking new ground, and recognising the new things that God was doing. They were the missionary pioneers (Acts 8:1, 14; 11:1,18).

● *The maturity of the church.* In Ephesians 4:11 we are told that God gave the ministry gifts of apostles, prophets, pastors and teachers to equip the saints and to build up the church. Apostles are not the managing directors at the top of the spiritual pyramid; rather they are the servants of the heavenly maker and builder.

Thus the ministry of the apostles is both foundational and functional. Insofar as the foundations of the church have been laid, and do not need to be laid again, the

ministry of the apostles—and thus the need for apostles
—has ended. But insofar as the church will still be
maturing until Jesus returns, the apostolic ministry of
Ephesians 4:11 will be required.

And that brings us to the heart of the matter. While
we cannot repeat or continue the unique and foundational ministry of the twelve apostles, we do need the
continuing functional ministry of the apostles for the
maturity of the church today. Does it exist, and if so
where and how?

The marks of the apostle

Quite clearly our fellow-Christians in the house church
movement believe they are right in recognising some of
their leaders as apostles. These people are not elected
or called; rather they are appointed in recognition of
the trans-local church ministry they have been given by
the Lord. In other parts of the Christian church a similar ministry is needed, and should—I believe—be recognised even if such Christian leaders are not termed
apostles. Local superintendents, district moderators
and Anglican bishops all have the ministry of linking
the churches together, understanding pioneer situations
where initiatives can be taken and acting as kindly older
brothers, whose objective view of a local church will
enable it to assess itself and correct any imbalance or
error in its life. They will seek always to bring that
church, in fellowship with others, to the maturity of
faith and life that the Lord intends for it.

Surely the Lord intends the ministry of the apostle
mentioned in Ephesians 4:11—whether people are
given the title or not—to continue until he returns.

Are elders essential to church leadership?

One of the best illustrations of a father-in-law's wisdom is that of the counsel given by Jethro to his son-in-law Moses (Exodus chapter 18). The responsibility of leading God's people had grown too heavy for Moses, and he was advised to choose capable men to share the work with him: an early example of shared leadership!

Jesus sent his disciples out in twos and the apostles selected seven deacons (Acts chapter 6) to share the administration. Elders are always mentioned in the plural in the Epistles—except where an individual elder is being warned concerning his conduct (see Acts 14:23; 20:17; 1 Timothy 5:17; Titus 1:5; James 5:14; 1 Peter 5:1).

The value of corporate leadership is many-faceted. Those involved can share the vision and responsibilities and strengthen and support one another. Together, they should be able to discern God's purposes more clearly, exercise a variety of gifts, help one another to be steady and persistent in prayer and stand firm in the spiritual battle.

The concept of corporate eldership in some parts of the church today has been hidden but is being rediscovered. It is hidden in that the word priest used in the Church of England is derived from the word *presbuteros* which means presbyter or elder. The word bishop or *episcopos* has the idea of overseer or elder. Traditionally the Anglican church has not exercised a biblical eldership, but this is being restored. Responsibility and ministry are being shared. In some places, elders are specifically appointed; in others, men and women are fulfilling an eldership role without any specific title.

If we are to see the church in any place grow, there needs to be shared ministry. If we expect more sheep, we shall need more shepherds. It is a demanding role (you can read about the responsibilities laid on elders in 1 Timothy chapter 3; Titus chapter 1; 1 Peter chapter 5; Hebrews chapter 13).

Let's welcome elders into our church—if we have not already done so. Let's encourage rather than criticise them. Above all, let's pray for them and love them in Christ. The minister can function as a one-man-band. But I believe that the New Testament teaches that we will not function effectively as churches without the shared leadership which eldership represents.

I attend a fellowship where dancing is sometimes included in the worship and I find this very unhelpful. What should I do?

This is a sensitive issue for many Christians—and not only for the older people who have been in the church for years. Like other elements in our worship—hymn tunes, the way prayers are led, the singing of choruses—dancing gets a mixed reception. We may thrill to or shudder at the sight of bishops dancing around the high altar in Canterbury Cathedral or the request to join in some informal jigging in the evening service.

What does the reluctant worshipper do? Go home, determined never to come again, or what?

May we widen the question slightly: What should leaders and congregation alike do over dance in worship?

We need to recognise that most people bring some cultural baggage and pre-conditioning to their worship. Some Christians have been brought up to think of dancing as wrong, worldly and having dangerous sexual overtones and therefore not to be included in worship; others may see it as an innocent form of bodily expression.

Read the Scriptures and find out what they teach about dancing. Herodias' dancing was clearly carnal and wrong (Matthew 14:6; Mark 6:22); David's dancing before the Lord offended his wife (2 Samuel 6:16); but the psalmist calls upon us to worship the Lord with our whole being and that clearly could include dancing (Psalm 103:1; 149:3 and 150:4). Dancing was one of the ways in which Christians expressed their joy and delight before the Lord and with each other at what God had done (Luke 15:25).

Leaders must be wise when introducing or allowing dance within worship, and patient in explaining the meaning of movements so that these can edify people and glorify the Lord. Dance can be used as a formal part of the worship with a properly trained and rehearsed team (rather like a choir or music group), who seek to express visibly with their bodies what others may be expressing verbally or through music.

Dance can also be used informally. Freedom can be given to individual members of the congregation to express their worship in dance, provided always that one person's freedom doesn't become another person's stumbling-block. What is appropriate for people to do in the privacy of their own homes may not be appropriate in corporate worship. For example, the fact that it is perfectly acceptable for a housewife to dance, sing and praise, while listening to a tape in the privacy of her kitchen, doesn't *necessarily* justify everyone doing the same thing in church. And it would seem unwise and unloving to impose dance on a congregation as well as quite wrong to suggest that if people don't join in, this would indicate a coolness of spirit on their part!

Remember that we are members one of another—called to love and encourage one another. So when something happens in worship that we find unhelpful, we should not complain and criticise, for that only gives Satan a foothold to divide what Christ has joined together. Rather, thank God that there are some in the church who are able to worship the Lord in dance, while admitting that this isn't the case for us. There will always be elements in worship that help one person and hinder others.

Speaking personally, I haven't always found dance helpful—though my wife is a trained ballet teacher! However, sometimes—for example, when dance has been used to interpret a familiar hymn, such as 'Alleluia, give thanks to the risen Lord'—I have been deeply moved by it. So have others, including visitors. But not everyone has felt the same way. Whatever we do or don't do, we won't please everyone. Our aims should be to please the Lord while loving and accepting one another in him.

Should we move to another church? Our minister preaches that the spiritual gifts went out with the early church and all the deacons, except one, agree with him!

Many people will echo this personal, painful and difficult question. Whenever Christians who are open to the Spirit of God gather at renewal conferences, this is an issue that is raised. The renewal movement itself has become divided between those who teach and urge that we stay in our main-line churches whatever happens and others who believe that God is calling people out of

the main-line denominations into churches totally open
to the renewing work of the Spirit.

I would like to reply to this question by sharing the
testimony of a couple who have faced this issue.

Fred and Eileen write: 'We have been asked many
times over very many years why we don't move, since
the Holy Spirit is quenched in our church. The answer
is simple. *God has not told us to go!*

'My personal testimony of healing has made no
difference to the refusal of our leaders to believe that
the spiritual gifts are for today. We have suffered frustration, and wept as we have seen barrenness and futile
"human effort" in the church. *Now*, we praise God that
he has led us out of the wilderness of frustration and *set
us free within*. We remain in the church encouraging as
we have opportunity. Despite the situation at "the top",
the Lord is working at the grass roots.

'We simply asked God to deliver us from our frustration and *use us* for counselling and spiritual encouragement from within the church *and* from elsewhere.

'We continue to pray that we will be in the right place
at the right time, willing and available. God is doing
some amazing things and we can't praise him enough
for this freedom—even though we remain in a spiritually
stifled church. We constantly pray for our minister and
each deacon that they will know the true joy of the
Lord within and stop struggling in human strength. We
pray for the headship of Christ in the fellowship. To
God be the glory!'

I believe that testimony will be a real encouragement
to others in similar situations. I'm sure that God will
answer such prayers and that some time in the future
that church will burst open into spiritual life through
the work of God's Spirit.

The key to answering the question: 'Should we move

to another church?' lies in answering another question: 'Has God told you to go?' If he has—go; if he hasn't—stay.

3

Spiritual Gifts and Signs and Wonders

What are spiritual gifts and what is their purpose?

One of St Paul's favourite descriptions of the church is the body of Christ. He is comparing the church to a human body. Just as the human body is directed, empowered and motivated by the head, so the church should be led and guided by its head—the Lord Jesus Christ. Just as the physical body should act and move in a harmonious and united way, so should the church. Sadly, this is not always true. But as we understand more about the gifts and learn to allow Jesus to act through his church by way of the gifts, this will become more and more true. Putting it as simply as we can, the gifts of the Spirit refer to the action of the risen Lord in and through his body the church.

The definition of the gifts
There are various lists and descriptions of the gifts in the New Testament letters—the four crucial passages being Romans chapter 12; 1 Corinthians chapter 12; Ephesians chapter 4 and 1 Peter chapter 4. It is helpful to notice that the context of every passage is that of Christ's love in his body, so the Bible doesn't separate

the gifts of the Spirit—what God does: his conduct—from the fruit of the Spirit—God's character: what he is like. If God doesn't make this separation or place more emphasis on one than the other, neither should we.

The purpose of the gifts
The gifts are given for three purposes:

● So that the church can minister to itself (Ephesians 4:11). Some of the gifts—such as those for apostles, prophets, teachers, pastors and evangelists—are the gifts of the risen Christ to enable the rest of the body—the saints—to fulfil the work of ministry.
● This work of ministry was to bring about the growth and maturity of the body. When Paul writes to the Ephesians (4:13–15), he describes the different stages of growth in the church as infancy, growing up as teenagers and on to adulthood or maturity. So what is true in physical life should also be true in spiritual experience. The gifts are for ministry leading to maturity.
● The gifts are also for mission and evangelism. We must never forget that the church exists for mission in the world and for the glory of God. It never exists for its own well being. So gifts are given that the church may be outward-reaching, and upward-looking, as well as steadily maturing. To that end, God will work by his Spirit within his body.

You will find in 1 Corinthians 12:4–7 that Paul uses different words to describe the work of God's Spirit. If we look at each word very briefly in turn, we can build up an identikit picture of the gifts.

● 'There are different kinds of gifts'—*charismata* (v.4). The origin and source of the variety of gifts is *God*. So we can never feel we have earned or merited any gift. It is given as a sign of God's undeserved love and grace to every one of us.

● There are different kinds of service—*diakonia* (v.5). The word reveals that these gifts will minister to the very many different needs of people. For example, people will need teaching, encouragement, a word of wisdom, practical help, leadership or pastoral care. Just as the needs vary, so will the gifts that are provided to meet those needs.

● There are different kinds of working—*energmaton* (v.6). The outworking and effects of the gifts—the expression of the gifts—will be varied.

● There will be the manifestation of the Spirit—*phanerosis* (v.7). The gifts will be made visible and real in what is the invisible but real power of the Spirit. You may have noticed that God—Father, Son and Holy Spirit—are linked in this passage, so the Trinity is associated with the gifts.

In summary, the gifts are the various and different ways in which God by his grace acts through every part of his body to meet visibly the special needs of others; or, as someone has put it: 'A spiritual gift is a special attribute given by the Holy Spirit to every member of the body of Christ according to God's grace for use within the context of the body.'

Important distinctions about the gifts

A spiritual gift is not the same as a natural talent. Natural talent may be the seed-bed that nurtures the gift but, whereas a talent stems from our abilities and personalities, a gift is derived from the grace of the Lord.

The gifts of the Spirit are not the same as the fruit of the Spirit. You can see that as you compare the lists of the fruit in Galatians chapter 5 with any of the lists of the gifts of the Spirit mentioned above. The gifts are linked to what we do and the fruit to what we are. Gifts are distinct; not everyone has every gift, but everyone has at least one. The fruit appears gradually and everyone is a branch on which all the fruit appear.

We can also make a distinction between having a gift and having a ministry or office. A person may receive a word of prophecy without having a prophetic ministry or office. However, if a person regularly exercised a prophetic gift, the church might consider recognising that he had a prophetic ministry and allowing him to fulfil a prophetic office. Similarly, those called to any office should have the appropriate gifts and ministry. For example, those called to teach and pastor should be people who clearly have the gifts and ministries of teaching and pastoring.

It is important to distinguish between general responsibilities and the exercise of specific gifts. The New Testament teaches that while every Christian has the responsibility to give, only some may have the gift of liberality. Again, we are all called to be witnesses, but some will have the gift of the evangelist.

Difficulties about the gifts
There are some difficulties that people have with the gifts. These are usually along one of the two lines.

● *Difficulties in attitudes towards gifts*. When Paul wrote to the Corinthians (1 Corinthians 12:14ff.) he was aware that some of the Christians were proud and boasting of their gifts as if they were superior to others. Other Christians in the same church, however, were feeling very inferior with their gifts. Paul has to rebuke the Corinthian church for this unspiritual attitude.

Sadly, the same can still be true. We must remember that every gift we have is given by God and must be used in love and not in pride.

● *Difficulties in accepting some of the gifts.* It is not easy to compile a complete and final list of all the gifts. People used to say there were nine gifts of the Spirit; now the list has lengthened to about twenty-seven: and it is generally accepted that leading in worship, being a missionary and enduring martyrdom are not included in the New Testament lists but should be.

The main area of contention in the church concerns whether the more spectacular gifts mentioned in 1 Corinthians chapter 12 died out with the apostles and the early church or are available today. In the light of the growing testimony around the world, and the increasing numbers of local churches and fellowships experiencing the release of God's gifts, it is much harder to hold that these gifts don't exist today. We can be on firmer ground from the Bible, however. I believe that it teaches that all the gifts are for today, so we can believe this on biblical grounds rather than simply on the evidence all around us. The Greek verbs in 1 Corinthians chapter 12 are in the continuous present, suggesting continuous availability. We must not pick and choose what we believe in the Bible, cutting out 1 Corinthians chapters 12 and 14 and keeping in 1 Corinthians chapters 11, 13 and 15, for example.

To me it seems clear that God is graciously bearing testimony by his own Spirit to the truth of the gifts for today. Others may not see things in the same way. All of us must remember that we are members of the same body of Christ and that we are to hold one another— and the truth—in love. Don't let's fall out over the gifts when we are united in Jesus.

Can you please give me guidance about the ministry of the laying on of hands?

Most people's experience of the laying on of hands is limited to having the bishop's hands placed on one's head during the confirmation service or a clergyman's hands laid on in the 'blessing' of children at the communion rail. Some may have had hands laid on them when they were sick, or seen this done to others.

The Holy Spirit has been restoring this gracious ministry *through* and *for* more and more people. It is a ministry often referred to in the Scriptures.

It is a sign of general blessing and assurance. For example, Jacob blessed his grandsons, Jesus blessed the children brought to him and Ananias blessed Saul following his conversion (Genesis 48:14–16; Mark 10:16; Acts 9:17).

It is used when commissioning people for specific tasks. It is an outward symbol of the church's authorisation. This was true for the Levites in their work in the Temple, for Moses and Joshua, for the seven deacons, for Paul and Barnabas when they were sent off on their first missionary journey and for Timothy in his work in leading the church at Ephesus (see Numbers 8:10; 27: 15–23; Deuteronomy 34:9; Acts 6:1–5; 13:1–3; 1 Timothy 4:14). I believe we can use the ministry of laying on of hands more than we do, to commission and authorise all kinds of lay workers in our church. I am sure that having hands laid on is greatly confirming to those who are taking up new work or even re-dedicating themselves to existing work.

The ministry of the laying on of hands is clearly linked with prayer for those who are sick. It helps those who are ill to know that those praying for them are closely identified with them; and, since we are instructed to lay hands on those who have specifically asked for this ministry, it is a means of strengthening and affirming their faith. We find that Jesus often laid hands on those who were sick; on one occasion, because of the unbelief that was all around him, it was the only thing that he was able to do (see Matthew 9:18; Mark 5:23; 6:5; 16:18; Luke 13:13).

It was also through the laying on of hands that people received the Holy Spirit (see Acts 8:17; 19:6). Don't misunderstand what the Bible is saying. The reception of the Holy Spirit was not automatic because hands were laid on; rather the laying on of hands indicated that the person was willing and ready to receive from God and also that God was longing to give.

We need also to be clear about the right practice of this ministry. Paul warns Timothy to lay hands suddenly on no man (1 Timothy 5:22). When friends are praying privately for one another, I am sure that it is acceptable for them to lay hands on one another if this is appropriate and wanted. When the ministry is being exercised on an official public occasion, it would seem right that some control and authorisation should be recognised. Such public ministry should be exercised only by those who have been ordained, those elected to certain offices in the church or those whose gifts and ministry to others have been publicly recognised.

In the past, the ministry of the laying on of hands has probably been restricted to too few occasions and to too narrow a circle of people. The Holy Spirit is restoring this gracious work to fuller use by a wider group of Christian people. Let's make way for him to minister in this way amongst us.

How do I know what gifts I have been given?

This is probably among the top ten questions people want to ask. I would like to offer eight pointers to anyone wanting to know what gifts he has been given.

● Understand that every born-again Christian has at least one spiritual gift. There will be gifts that we *don't* have. Knowing what gifts we haven't got can be just as liberating as knowing what gift(s) we have been given (see 1 Corinthians 12:7; Romans 12:6; Ephesians 4:6; 1 Peter 4:10). Such gifts are expressions of God's grace and not the reward for merit or long service in the church.

● Review the gifts that are available. Some of the gifts are apparently based on natural abilities: teaching, pastoring, administration, caring, helping. Others are more obviously supernatural gifts: tongues, interpretations and prophecy. The two groups of gifts (some would call the first group ministries and the second, gifts) are complementary. The first list defines the sort of work we are called to do in the church; the second, the spiritual gifts God gives us as we fulfil our ministry. In the case of gifts such as having words of wisdom or knowledge, we are to use them and pass them on. We don't store up those gifts; we are merely the channels— not the reservoirs—that God chooses to use.

● Live and walk in the Spirit. The passages referred to have much to say about our relationships with our fellow-believers; if these are not right, we shall block what God wants to give to us. We learn from 1 Corinthians 12:3 that the confession that Jesus is Lord is the key to understanding and releasing the gifts of the Spirit.

● Submit to the fellowship. The gifts are usually discovered within the fellowship of a small group. Friends will tell us they believe we have such and such a gift. The leadership of the church or of the group will again be in a position to help fellow-Christians find their gifts. I wonder whether you have given time and opportunity in your fellowship groups to prayerfully consider the gifts and ministries that God's Spirit has given to every member of the group. Why not try that exercise? It will release all the members to fulfil the roles God has for them, and lead to the growth of the group and the church.

● Prayerfully consider the possibilities—just as, in a restaurant, you would look at the menu before you ate. What do you think you are good at? What do you enjoy doing? What are you not good at? Do you enjoy ministry among older people? Teaching the children? Organising the parish church weekend houseparty? Welcoming people at the church door? Working on the church's newsletter? In times of worship do you sense God is giving you a word of knowledge, or a word of prophecy?

● Be willing to use the gifts which you think God has given you (1 Corinthians 12:31; 14:1; 2 Timothy 4:6–8). Fear is the real enemy that holds us back, but the Holy Spirit is not the Spirit of fear. It will be in the small group, first of all, that we should find a loving and accepting arena in which to try out the gifts. You will discover what works and what doesn't. Rather like a member of a football team, you will soon know which position you play best in. Sometimes it happens that a football manager, after a season or two, wants a player to switch to a new position. Sometimes God does that with us: he redirects our ministry or gives us different gifts for his body.

● Test the gifts (1 Thessalonians 5:21), not least by using them. You—and others—will easily confirm whether you are right for Sunday School teaching, visiting people in hospital, helping in the church office, or whatever.

• Cover the whole exercise in prayer and don't be anxious.

My friend has the gift of tongues. Is this a gift I should seek?

We are to earnestly desire the spiritual gifts—of which tongues is one (1 Corinthians 14:1; 12:10). God gives his love-gifts to his children, and tongues will help us in our prayer and praise, and in our battle against Satan. Christians may receive the gift of tongues when they first know the full release of the Spirit, but that is not always the case, and nowhere does the New Testament insist that tongues is the sign that you have the fulness or baptism of the Spirit.

There are some dangers to avoid. Don't seek 'tongues' as a status symbol. On the other hand, don't take the passive attitude that you are willing to receive the gift if God wants to give it to you. We are commanded to earnestly seek the spiritual gifts, and that implies a personal, active, deep spiritual desire to receive everything God wants to share with us. Above all it is essential that we seek the giver—the Lord Jesus—and not just his gifts.

There are various practical steps to help you seek. Some Christians have sought and received while on their own, after a period of reading and praying, and have found that a fount of praise, released within them, just continues to bubble up in a new heavenly language. Others have asked a Christian friend or minister to pray for them; at first nothing seems to happen; then they are given (and say aloud) a few words they don't understand and they may even wonder whether they are making them up. Don't be put off if this is happening to you. Persist. Use the language, however strange and limited it may be, and God will release more and more to you. Then, go on using the gift as Scripture directs—notice the distinction between the private and public use of tongues (1 Corinthians 14:2–4, 13–15, 26–27).

What if nothing happens? Don't worry, trust God, for it is his sovereign gift to give as and when he chooses. One person I know told me that it was ten years after he had first sought tongues that God fully answered his prayer. We may not have to wait as long as he did!

What are signs and wonders? Should we expect God to work through them in the church today, or did they die out with the early church, as I have heard other Christian teachers claim?

Until about four or five years ago, most of us were unfamiliar with the concept of signs and wonders. Especially through the ministry of John Wimber from The Vineyard Ministries in California, God has been teaching thousands of Christian leaders and members around the world more about the supernatural work of the Kingdom of God. The ministries of some have been transformed or enriched. Yet others in the body of Christ have written and spoken against this. Let me share with you what I understand of the Bible's teaching about signs and wonders.

The meaning of signs and wonders
Four main words are used in the New Testament to describe the work of God in people's lives.

● Signs—*semia*. This word is mainly used in John's Gospel. John writes of the seven great signs—such as the feeding of the five thousand, the turning of water into wine at the wedding in Cana. He also speaks of the eighth great sign who is Jesus himself (John 2:18ff.).
● Wonders—*terrata*. This is a word that describes the wonderful works of the Lord (see, for example: Acts 2:43; 4:30; 5:12; 6:8; 7:36; 14:3; Romans 15:19; 2 Corinthians 12:12; Hebrews 2:4).
● Power—*dunamis*. This describes an act of power or miracle in the ministry of Jesus (Luke 4:14, 36; 5:17; 9:1; 10:19).
● Works—*erga*. This describes the activity of God (John 5:20; 5:36; 9:4).

From this very sketchy review one thing should be abundantly clear. Signs and wonders describe what God does, and not what man does. They therefore reveal and reflect not the weak attempt of men, but the powerful activity and presence of the living God. Such manifestations may refer to healings, the demonstration of the Spirit of God through the gifts of the Spirit or the visible visitation of the Spirit on a group of Christians.

The demonstration of signs and wonders
So far in our answer there need be no controversy within the church. The controversial issue concerns whether or not God works today in the ways in which he worked in the past.

● *The work of God the Father in the Old Testament:*

There are lots of references to signs and wonders in both the Psalms and the historical books of the Old Testament. They relate especially to God's activity at the time of the Exodus, and the return of God's people from captivity in Babylon.

● *The work of the Son in the Gospels:* There are more than forty healings recorded in the Gospels; the extraordinary events of three people raised from the dead and the woman who touched the hem of Jesus' clothes and was cured; the nature miracles—calming the storms, cursing the fig tree and feeding the five thousand; various instances of exorcism and deliverance.

● *The work of the Spirit in the Acts of the Apostles and the early church.* The Holy Spirit manifests himself through tongues, healings, prophecies, deliverance and the casting out of evil spirits.

Does God work similarly today? Some take the view that signs and wonders stopped with the apostolic age. My contention is that we are to make way for the Spirit in the church today: make way for his gifts and also for his power expressed through signs and wonders. A review of church history would show—I believe— that God has never ceased to work through signs and wonders where he can find open and willing people through whom to act. Jesus also promised us that what he had begun to do, God would continue through his church (John 5:19; 14:12). Our faith is Trinitarian. You will notice that the three persons of the Trinity are all involved in this ministry.

Some warnings about signs and wonders
Jesus warned people about the dangers of seeking signs for the sake of the signs themselves (see Matthew 12: 38–39; 16:2–4; John 2:18–22). We are not free from this

same danger and temptation in the healing ministry today.

Signs can be counterfeited. Remember the magicians in Exodus, and the miracle-workers in the days of Jesus (Matthew 7:22; Mark 13:22). So we should not be surprised to find that Satan—who can turn himself into an angel of light, and who is the father of lies—can also use people to imitate what God alone can do.

Signs and wonders won't always promote faith. We are warned about this through the ministry of Jesus (see John 6:26 and Luke 16:30–31). The same is sadly true today. People can see and hear about others being miraculously healed without turning in faith to Christ for salvation.

The misuse of the ministry of signs and wonders should not lead to their disuse but should prompt us to the right use of this ministry.

Right expectations about signs and wonders
The right context, according to the New Testament, is that of mission. The disciples and the apostles were determined to preach the good news of the Kingdom, to focus upon the person of Jesus, and to go with no other message than that of Jesus and him crucified (Matthew 10:7; Luke 10:9; 1 Corinthians 1:18). It should be in the on-going work of mission that God will manifest his power through signs and wonders. This will work out in two special ways.

Signs and wonders can open the door for evangelism and promote faith and expectancy (see Acts 8:6–8; 14: 8–10). Dr Donald McGavran, who has devoted his life to mission and church growth, has testified: 'I now hold that among vast populations, divine healing is one of the ways in which God brings men and women to believe in the Saviour.' Also, signs and wonders can confirm the preaching and message of the gospel (see Mark 16:16, 20; 1 Corinthians 2:4–5; Hebrews 2:4).

I would humbly testify that this has been our experience. Although we are still learners, longing for God to do much more among us, and although he still has much to teach us, the ministry of signs and wonders is real and effective among us today. Individuals and whole families have come to personal faith because of what God has done in their lives. Signs and wonders have opened the way for and also confirmed the preaching of the gospel.

While we rejoice, we need constantly to hold the right balance between our weakness and God's power. Speaking at Acts '86, Canon Michael Green rightly summed up what our attitude should be when he said: 'Charismatic Christianity has concentrated too much on the power and the glory and the sense of having arrived. A realistic Christianity is neither defeatist nor triumphalist. It holds fast to the weakness of our frail human condition and to the glory of the Lord in our midst.

'Expect the Holy Spirit to work in power among you, but never forget you are in a world subject to suffering, sin and to the death.'

We are wanting to introduce the ministry of healing and signs and wonders into our church, but we are not sure how to start. Can you help us?

As I write this, it is just over three years since we introduced a similar ministry in our own church, and God has graciously used it to minister to people, to bring healing, to extend the evening congregation, and to bring men and women to faith in Jesus. We have much to praise the Lord for, and I pray that you will find at least the same joy and blessing in taking this step of faith.

May I share with you in some detail what this ministry has meant for us.

The foundations to be laid
It is vital to spend time making sure that very firm foundations are laid for this ministry. Let me mention ten vital foundation stones—none of which can really be neglected.

● Make sure in your own mind that the ministry of healing, and of signs and wonders is biblical. (Paul mentions it almost in passing in Acts 14:3, Romans 15:18–19 and 1 Corinthians 2:4.) The context of this ministry is mission (Luke 10:1, 19–21). Signs and wonders can open the door for evangelism, or they can confirm the message of the gospel that has been preached (Acts 8:6–8; 14:8ff.; Mark 16:16–20).

● The ministry we are concerned with is the work and ministry of the Holy Spirit. It is his work and we are just God's messengers. We read in Luke 5:17 that the power of the Lord was present to heal, and that power is often released through the gifts of the Spirit.

● We must be ready for the spiritual battle that will accompany this ministry. We are going to be involved in the power encounter between the Kingdom of God and light, and the Kingdom of Satan and darkness. Thus our personal relationship with the Lord is crucial (see Matthew 4:23; 9:35; Luke 4:1; 13–14).

● The Lord longs that people should become whole people (Matthew 22:37ff.). We are to love the Lord our God with all our heart, soul, strength and mind. Thus we shall become involved not only in the healing of the body, but also in the healing of past hurts, in inner healing, in deliverance ministry and in all that makes for wholeness of the personality through Christ.

● We have to establish the absolute priority of prayer in the work—whether as a personal or corporate ministry. (For us, the prayer time from 5.45 p.m. to 6.15 p.m. before the evening service is an absolute must. It is a time when faith is quickened, words of knowledge are received, and we are equipped by God.) We have had to learn that if we are going to minister to the needs and vulnerability of others, we have to be willing for God and others to minister to our needs and vulnerability first.

● We would strongly urge you to gain the support of your P.C.C. or church leadership. We found it was time well spent to share an outline of the biblical teaching with our church leadership and to be open about all things. We needed to assure our leaders that we were not jumping on the latest Christian band-wagon; but, rather, that we had discovered new and neglected biblical truth. It might be helpful for me to share the wording of the following resolution which was passed unanimously by our Parochial Church Council: 'The P.C.C. endorses the healing ministry within the church and seeks to call out and help equip members of the congregation to share in that ministry.'

● Teach about the ministry from the Bible as fully as you can. This is valuable for the whole congregation as well as for potential team members. Satan loves to spread rumour, lies and uncertainty, and the only adequate response to his work is the teaching of the truth of God's word.

● The best context for the ministry of healing in church is worship. We found that we had to make more and more space for God to be worshipped and to speak through words of knowledge and 'pictures'. Worship leads us into the presence of God, and in his presence there is power.

● Be ready to step out in faith—especially in response to words of knowledge—but be careful to explain what you expect to happen and why you are inviting God's Holy Spirit to come and minister.

● If you don't already do so, value the ministry of the body in love very highly. One of the tasks of leaders is to equip others for the work of ministry (Ephesians 4:11–13; 1 Corinthians 12:12; 1 Peter 4:8–10).

I have found it important to take time to lay the right foundations. It is equally essential to discover the people whom God is calling out and equipping to share in this ministry. Our testimony is that where people have wrongly been invited into the team, they have soon fallen out and others, whom God has been calling but who have been hesitating diffidently, have then come forward. Team members, we believe, should have particular qualities or attitudes in common.

Features of team members
In seeking to discover whom God was calling to this ministry, we held two teaching meetings and two more informal suppers to teach about the ministry and to explain the kind of people God would be calling out. Later, we found it important to keep the team together through regular times of fellowship and worship and encouragement while, at the same time, keeping open to those who might come to feel that God was drawing them into this ministry.

We feel that the team members should:

- Accept the healing ministry today in its fulness.
- Have a vital relationship with Jesus—just as Jesus did with the Father (John 5:17–21).
- Be open to all the work of the Holy Spirit, and believe in his supernatural work.
- Be motivated by compassion and long to see the Kingdom of God extended over sickness and the lack of wholeness in people (Luke 4:18; 39).
- Be spiritually mature and have rounded personalities, since their ministry will involve spiritual battles and be demanding and costly. Being willing for others to minister to them would help them to mature and prepare them for ministry to others.
- Be invited and authorised by the minister, submitting to his leadership and working under his authority or those appointed by him. It should be made clear that people are not automatically involved in the ministry because of any office they hold, or because their husband or wife has been commissioned.
- Be open to the gifts of the Spirit, and willing to share as God gives words of knowledge or releases his gifts amongst his people.
- Receive training in their ministry.
- Be people who can, normally, come to the times of prayer and preparation before times of ministry.
- Be members of the body of Christ and members of one another, having a right attitude to each other as well as to the Lord (Romans 12:3ff.).

Once we had stepped out on this ministry we were to face both fears and fruit. I'm not suggesting that it will be exactly the same for others, but it might encourage —as well as warn—if I share what our fears and joys were.

The fears to be faced

● The fear of failure; the fear that people will not respond or that there will not be a continuing need for the ministry. I'd like to encourage you not to be discouraged by small beginnings (see Exod 23:29–30; Zechariah 4:6, 8, 10). Once we got going, we found that we did not have enough people available during the weekdays to minister to the needs that began to be revealed!

● The fear that people will ridicule—mainly a fear that church people rather than outsiders would mock. I was especially embarrassed at first to give out words of knowledge, fearing that people might think we had made them up. However, they were often so different week by week to meet specific situations that gradually it became exciting to discover what God was doing amongst us.

● The fear of being thought odd or going overboard. As the ministry becomes established and recognised within the life of the local church, the pendulum will settle, the spotlight will not be so fiercely upon this ministry, and it will be regarded as an essential element in the work. Remember that our full ministry is to save and to serve men and women.

● The fear of elitism—i.e. that there is something very special about those who pray for healing. We need to deal with this by showing that the ministry of teaching in the Sunday School or singing in the choir is just as important.

● The fear of being vulnerable to God and to others. Those of us who are trained to give out, have to learn to receive and be open to God and others.

The fruit to be expected

● All sorts of blessings and healings in people's lives.

- Opportunities for evangelism and people committing themselves to Jesus.
- A deepening fellowship in the Spirit with others involved in the ministry.
- Growth in our own lives spiritually and experientially.

It might be helpful for me to suggest some other matters requiring attention.

Follow-on to be planned
- We found that there was a constant need to enlarge the team and train others—especially men. This was essential within a year of making a start.
- A ministry of counselling in greater depth developed during the weekdays. We had to make a distinction between equipping people to minister in the power of the Spirit through the prayer ministry, and equipping them for a greater in-depth counselling ministry with more emphasis on deliverance or inner healing.
- This naturally underlined the need for continuing training. We built up a tape-library, and shared various jobs around the team. We ensured that all new people coming into the ministry had listened to the basic John Wimber tapes on signs and wonders and also encouraged people to come to the monthly Saturday morning teaching seminars that were arranged for our own church and other churches and fellowships in the area.
- Thought needs to be given to sharing the ministry with others.

The one thing that is certain about this ministry of healing and signs and wonders is that you never know where God will lead you next!

What is the biblical basis for the ministry of inner healing?

This is a very important question and here are some general guidelines.

The meaning of inner healing

Healing is wholeness. 'The human being is an inter-related, interconnected and interdependent unity of body, soul (mind, memories and emotions) and spirit. What happens in one part will inevitably affect the other parts sooner or later' (page 29, *Healing is for the Whole Person*, Barbara Pursey).

Inner healing, or healing of past hurts, refers to what other people—often those near to us—have done to us. Healing may be needed to deal with bitterness, resentment, rejection, anger or guilt. As a person reacts in the inner man (the mind, will, heart, emotions or spirit) so these reactions will affect other parts of our being.

The vital distinction between the practice of inner healing and the insights that other disciplines may bring to the same problem is that Christian inner healing not only exposes the need but also applies the truths of the Christian gospel—acceptance, forgiveness, meaning and purpose in life—to the troubled areas. In this way, inner healing will differ from some group therapies, T-groups and pyschotherapy. It certainly will have nothing to do with the practices of spiritism and the occult and many Christians are doubtful about the rightness of using hypnosis.

The Scriptural basis for inner healing

There are, I believe, six different aspects of biblical truth which relate to the ministry of inner healing:

• Salvation, like inner healing, is concerned with the

wholeness of a person. We are told that the word of God penetrates even to dividing the soul and spirit, joints and marrow; it judges the thoughts and attitudes of the heart (Hebrews 4:12).

• The Bible is concerned with the effect that one generation has on the next (Exodus 20:4–6). The whole history of David and Israel after David's sin with Bathsheba demonstrates this clearly. But the gospel is concerned with undoing the wrong caused through sin (Romans 5:12–21).

• The work of the cross: Jesus' death was to reverse every aspect of the damage caused through sin. Atonement, justification, reconciliation, deliverance from wrath, forgiveness are not just theological terms; they become pastoral and personal realities in this ministry; added to which Paul tells us that the cross was in the plan and purpose of God from before the foundation of the world (Ephesians chapter 1) so, while Jesus died at a point in history and a place in the world, the effects of his death are for everywhere, every person and every time.

• Breaking or binding Satan's power: This is often involved in the ministry of inner healing (see Psalm 118: 10–12; Matthew 12:29). Remember also that Christ came to bind up the broken-hearted and to heal their wounds (Isaiah 61:1; Psalm 147:3).

• The renewing of the mind is surely involved in the ministry of inner healing. From negative thoughts about oneself, the Holy Spirit enables us to think positively (Romans 12:1–2; Ephesians 4:22–24).

• There are examples of people healed inwardly in the gospels. What about the woman at the well in John chapter 4? Why did Jesus ask Peter three times over a charcoal fire whether he loved him, if it wasn't to deal with Peter's three-fold denial and guilt (John 21:17;

Mark 14:72)? If ever there was a man who might have needed inner healing it was Joseph, when we remember what others had done to him, but he was able to see this from God's viewpoint (Genesis 45:4–8; 50:20).

I hope that this short summary of the biblical basis will help us to see that the ministry of inner healing is one very relevant aspect of pastoral care and evangelism. We have found that a number of people coming to us for ministry have received not only healing but the Saviour himself, and have become valuable members of the fellowship.

But things don't always work out as straightforwardly as this. For example, sometimes those who have been ministered to in this way seem to need intensive help and counselling afterwards. Our experience suggests that these should not be seen necessarily as resulting from inadequate ministry; they could be required by the very nature of the problem itself.

There are times, we have to admit, when we seem to have done nothing for a person. But we do also have to praise the Lord for other lives ransomed, healed, restored, forgiven. We still have much to learn and need constantly to seek the Lord for the right diagnosis and for his help in standing against Satan's subtle counter-attacks. Failure to have a one hundred per cent success rate doesn't invalidate either the ministry or the biblical basis of it. If it did, every aspect of the Christian ministry today would be invalidated since none could claim such a success rate!

Is it possible to lose one's healing?

The short answer is, 'Yes,' but we need to expand that by saying four things.

First, God wants us to be whole. Our health is part of God's salvation for us, and he has done all that is needed to make us perfectly whole. What God has begun, he will also complete. That is true of creation, redemption and salvation. From the cross there sounds out the shout of triumph: 'It is finished.'

Secondly, there are various reasons why healing may be incomplete or lost:

- *Disobedience*. If we continue in conscious sin at the same time as seeking God's healing, we are frustrating the purpose of God. We are to be holy because God is holy.
- *Doubt and unbelief*. Doubt is positively rejecting what God has promised to do and so frustrating what God has promised. 'He could not do any miracles there . . . He was amazed at their lack of faith' (Mark 6:5, 6).
- *Unwillingness to be fully healed*. Jesus asked the question, 'Do you want to be made whole' (John 5:6)? We can sometimes use illness as a crutch. It draws people's attention to us. Without sickness we would lose our special place in people's care.
- *Incorrect or incomplete diagnosis*. We are a whole person with a body, mind, spirit and emotions. They affect and interact with each other. The 'presenting' need may be bodily, but the real need may be for forgiveness (see the story of the paralysed man in Mark 2:1ff.). There will be incomplete or lost healing if we only patch up a life rather than root out a problem.
- *Ceasing to pray too soon*. Some healings are imme-

diate and complete. Others happen over a period of time. We can lose what has begun by ceasing to pray too soon.

● *Not following Scriptural directions.* Sometimes those who minister may hinder the healing process by not fully obeying the directions of Scripture in James 5:16; lack of healing may also be linked with indiscipline within the church (1 Corinthians 11:2–30).

● *Satanic counter-attack.* Remember, in the parable of the sower (Luke 8:12), Satan came and snatched away the word that had been given. He may try to snatch away the promises of healing that God has given to us. Again, Matthew 12:43–45 records an evil counter-attack after deliverance.

● *Faith on a false foundation.* You may even lose your healing because your faith is resting in some experience, or some other person, and not in the character and faithfulness of God. Make sure you go on trusting the Lord who is faithful.

Thirdly, whether we like it or not, we are all subject to disease, infection, the ageing process and even death. It is all part of our fallen humanity and of the creation being subject to decay (Romans 8:21).

Fourthly, you may be someone for whom healing hasn't yet begun, though you long for it, trust God for it, are walking in love and obedience with the Lord and know of no reason for your healing not coming. I can only point you to the cross as the supreme assurance of God's redeeming love for us and as the supreme demonstration of his power in us.

How can a Christian recognise and receive words of knowledge?

The only reference to words of knowledge is in the list of gifts of the Spirit (1 Corinthians 12:8) but there are numerous examples of this gift being used in both Old and New Testaments (1 Kings 19:14–18; 2 Kings 5:20–27; John 4:17; Acts 5:3). From these situations it is clear that a word of knowledge springs from knowledge that has not been acquired in the usual ways.

Some Christians would deny that words of knowledge are given today. They argue that they were given only in early church days. But against that view I would set 1 Corinthians chapters 12 and 14 and the experience of many Christians around the world who believe they are being given words of knowledge.[1]

I believe that they are a continuing gift of the Holy Spirit today. They may come as words impressed on our minds or as something seen with our spiritual eyes or identified by means of pain in a relevant part of our body. They are received as we are open and available to the Spirit of God, especially during a time of prayer or ministry. They should be shared with the appropriate person or persons at the appropriate time. God gives these words because he knows our wishes and needs and wants to bless us with his love and power.

1 See *Power Healing* (John Wimber, Hodder and Stoughton, 1986, Appendix D, p. 254) for a social anthropologist's analysis of words of knowledge.

Is it scriptural to talk about the Holy Spirit coming upon a person in the context of the healing ministry?

This is an issue that puzzles some Christians, especially those who have experienced the teaching and dramatic work of the Holy Spirit often associated with John Wimber. He, more than anyone else in the present day, has taught Christians to invite God the Holy Spirit to come and work in people's lives in many ways. I am sure that John, himself, would be the first to insist that we stick to Scripture, and find our authority for what we believe and do about the healing ministry in the Bible. Can we do that?

The simple answer is that there is very little evidence explicitly, for calling down the Holy Spirit in this particular manner, but there is a great deal of support implicitly for so doing. Let me summon five witnesses for us:

● The evidence of the ministry of Jesus himself is that he was filled with the Holy Spirit and that it was in the power of the Spirit that the Saviour healed (see Luke 4:14, 18; 5:17).
● The Holy Spirit acts as the executor of the Godhead.
Put very simply this means that what God the Father plans, and Jesus makes possible, the Holy Spirit applies and makes real. That is a general truth throughout the whole of the Bible and is particularly true in that gifts of healing are attributed to the Holy Spirit in 1 Corinthians 12:9. Thus we should expect the Holy Spirit to be at work in or upon people when the Lord is healing them.
● Certainly, this was the example of the ministry of the Holy Spirit in the Old Testament. We read of the Holy

Spirit coming upon a person for a particular work at a particular time. (There are a number of examples, but see Numbers 11:25; Judges 6:34; 11:29; 1 Samuel 10:10.)

● It was also the experience of the early church. There were clear outward and visible signs of the Spirit's presence and power (see Acts 2:4; 4:31) and the church had been taught to pray for the coming of the Holy Spirit in power (see Luke 11:13; John 14: 12–14). We often interpret the Bible in an individual sense, whereas these promises are given to the disciples meeting together. They were instructed to ask God to give more of his Spirit to them. No wonder things happened when they were around.

● A number of us would also have to testify that when we invite the Holy Spirit to come, God answers the prayer.

It is a bit unnerving to stand in front of our congregations and ask the Lord to send his Spirit in healing and blessing. Many of us have wondered what would happen if nothing happened! But our God is the God who does more than we desire or deserve. Seeing God at work will encourage your faith no end. So, if you are persuaded that such a prayer and practice is in harmony with the Scriptures and the mind of the Lord, may I exhort you to step out in faith. God won't let you down!

What is the prayer of faith?

In my Bible, the section James 5:13–18 is headed, 'The Prayer of Faith'. James is writing about the conduct to be followed by those who are in trouble, those who are happy or those who are sick. It is the responsibility of the sick person to call for the elders. They will come, anoint that person with oil, and pray, and the Lord will raise up the one who has been ill. Quite clearly, James is not limiting this ministry just to the apostles—it also applies to the spiritual leaders of our churches and fellowships today. Again, the writer certainly does not have in mind the Roman Catholic practice of extreme unction—which is sometimes justified by this passage. Rather than being a preparation for death, these verses are a prescription for life. James sees that alongside any medical ministrations, there is a place for the healing ministry of the church. So the prayer of faith is linked with the church's ministry of healing. Praise God that we are seeing that ministry being restored to the Christian church both within and outside of the renewal movement itself.

James is also describing the conditions to be fulfilled if there is to be healing. There really is no way round the promises in the second half of verse 15. Some would spiritualise by saying that they could refer to the person being raised up through the resurrection, but the original words do suggest physical well-being. The prayer of faith will make the sick person well. The Lord will raise him up. It seems from the context that faith is being exercised by the person who is ill—why otherwise would they call for the elders? It is certainly being demanded also of the elders themselves. Earlier (James 1:5–8) James has rebuked doubt in the heart of the person who asks. We cannot harbour doubt and faith in the same breath. James also realises that an unforgiving spirit can hinder both faith and healing. He wants all resentment and bitterness to be cleared out of the way. It has also been said that there must be no fear. Canon Jim Glennon who has held healing services and a healing ministry in Sydney, Australia, for more than twenty years once said, 'I have never known anyone healed who was afraid he would not be healed.' So the prayer of faith will be offered by the elders, in agreement with the person who is ill. There will be no place for doubt, fear, resentment or bitterness. It is quite clear that proper and helpful preparation for such prayer is essential. The people involved will want to ensure that there is no known and unconfessed sin in their lives. They may go through times of confession and repentance. They will certainly read the promises of the Bible and the stories of Jesus' healing ministry so that their faith will be stimulated.

But what is the nature and character of this faith about which James makes such a promise? With what sort of faith are we called to pray? James is not referring to mere human hope and trust—i.e. the sort of natural trust which believes a chair will support me when I sit upon it. He does not have in mind the faith exercised in salvation—faith in the grace of God by which we are justified. He is not talking about faith—or faithfulness—which is the fruit of the Spirit. Rather he is referring to the faith that God gives. I believe we would be right to equate this with the gift of faith. This is a faith that comes from God. We are called upon to work it out in prayer, rather than work it up in trembling hope.

Some people are given that gift of faith with which they pray on special occasions, knowing that God has heard and will answer. Other people—like Smith Wigglesworth for example—seem to be given that gift of faith for the whole of their ministry and marvellous stories are told of people healed through them.

If you feel that such an exercise of faith is beyond your ability at present, may we invite you to start trusting God for what you believe he can and will do in answer to your prayers. As you learn to trust him in the foothills of life, then you will find that you can trust him about the mountains!

I have faith but not the faith that removes mountains. Does that require the gift of faith? Should all Christians seek it?

It is important that we take our eyes off the mountains, and look at faith! The New Testament uses the word in different ways—such as the faith that saves or justifies us (Romans 3:2, 25, 26); the intellectual faith that even Satan has (James 2:19); and the faithfulness of God himself (Habakkuk 2:3–4; Hebrews 10:38).

The two key passages (1 Corinthians 13:2; Mark 11: 22–24) that link faith and mountains use faith in two different senses.

I'm sure that Paul in 1 Corinthians 13:2 means the gift of faith. He refers to faith, prophecy and knowledge, which must link back to the spiritual gifts in 1 Corinthians 12:8–10. Such spiritual gifts are given sovereignly by God, through his Spirit as and when the body or members of the body need them. For example, I believe that George Muller was given the gift of faith to fulfil the life of faith to which God had called him. If you look at the events recorded in such passages as John 11:41–42; Matthew 8:10; Acts 3:6, you will see Jesus, the centurion and Peter all responding to a particular situation with a gift of faith.

When we turn to Jesus' teaching in Mark 11:22–24 we find he is speaking about the conditions every believer is to fulfil all the time to enjoy the experience of answered prayer. Jesus is teaching us to put our faith neither in faith and the fact that we believe, nor in the fact that we have asked, but solely on the foundation of what he says. The basis of prayer must be the promises that God has given us in his word or by his Spirit. Jesus, therefore, exhorts his disciples (v.22) to have faith in God. What we should be seeking, according to Mark chapter 11, is not more faith in the same God but a greater understanding of God in whom we can have more faith. Praise helps here. As we magnify his name, so we enlarge our vision of the Lord, and trust him more.

A final thought: we must not rule out the very real possibility of the gift of faith. However, most of us need to learn to live by faith in God's promises. We need to stop being willing to settle for little answers to little prayers and set our sights on the Lord; for, as the angel said to Mary, 'Nothing is impossible with God.' Mary's reply was: 'I am the Lord's servant . . . May it be to me as you have said.' Instead of seeking the gift of faith, she allowed her soul to magnify the Lord and to rejoice in her Saviour. That's a very sensible example to follow.

How do we test the spirits?

It is possible to receive many conflicting messages in today's world. People press the claims of other religions and faiths; advertise the services of astrologers and mediums; lecture us on new world philosophies; preach the claims of Jesus. A cacophony of confusing creeds beats upon the ears of bemused men and women. How do we know what is true and what is false?

John, writing his first letter, faced a similar problem

in the ancient world, and he taught the church to test the spirits in order to know what was genuine and what was false (1 John 4:1). John was aware that many false prophets had gone out into the world and he was warning the believer against believing every spirit. (This shows that healthy scepticism can be a true mark of Christian maturity.)

The key test is, 'Do the spirits acknowledge that Jesus Christ has come in the flesh' (1 John 4:2, 3)? The word used implies that it is not just a matter of confession—of making some particular statement of faith—but of lifestyle based on the one in whom we actually believe and trust. It was possible for evil spirits to recognise that Jesus is the Son of God—Mark 1:24; 3:11, so obviously believing something about a person is different from believing in that person.

Because testing the spirits is very important, God has given his church the gift of spiritual discernment so that we might be guided into all the truth (1 Corinthians 12:10). 'The gift of discerning spirits gives to the church and its members the ability to distinguish between the divine, human and demonic powers' (*Gifts and Graces*, Arnold Bittlinger, Hodder and Stoughton, 1967, p. 45). In practical terms the Holy Spirit will bear witness with our spirit as to the genuine identity of a particular spirit. Some will try to parade as good—Satan disguises himself as an angel of light (2 Corinthians 11:14)—but God enables us to know the genuine from the false and to act accordingly.

What is praying in the Spirit?

If you have never experienced praying in the Spirit before, you may well feel a bit cautious about getting involved. In some ways it is like swimming. You can either walk around the swimming pool and dip your toes in the shallow end or you can swim in the deep end. Let me encourage you to dive in. Before you do, you ought to understand one or two things about praying in the Spirit—which some Christians define too narrowly and others too widely. (I have written fairly fully about this subject in my book *Prayer Changes People*, pp.48–61.)

First, praying in the Spirit is a principle in prayer. The New Testament makes it absolutely clear that we either live 'in the flesh' or 'in the Spirit'. Either we permit the world and self and our lower earthly nature to control and dictate to us, or we are to allow the Holy Spirit to direct our lives (see Romans 8:5–8; Galatians 5:16–17). Again and again the New Testament urges us to walk in the Spirit. In the same way we are to allow the Holy Spirit to direct our praying.

Let me share a picture with you. As Christians, we have two essential ambassadors active in our spiritual lives. There is the Lord Jesus as our ambassador—or advocate—before the Father's throne (1 John 2:1). Also, the Father has sent his ambassador—the Holy Spirit—the Comforter—into our hearts to represent the Father to us.

It is the Holy Spirit who will make real our relationship with the Father, through the saving work of the Lord Jesus; if he did not do this, our prayers would be dead, dreary and dull, only reaching the ceiling. It is when we are praying in the Spirit that our prayers reach the throne of God.

We also need our spiritual ambassador because we all have many weaknesses in prayer and we are tempted to give up too soon; we don't know what to pray for; we find it hard to trust God for his answer. So the Holy Spirit comes to help us in our praying (Romans 8:26–27).

Secondly, praying in the Spirit involves partnership in prayer. We are told on a number of occasions that we should pray in the Spirit (see Romans 8:26–27; Ephesians 6:18; Jude 20, 21). The Holy Spirit has particular ways in which he makes us aware of his help in prayer. Paul (Romans 8:26–27) speaks of groans and sighs and (1 Corinthians 12:7) of the utterance gifts of tongues because one of the lovely ways in which the Holy Spirit very specially helps us in prayer is through the gift of praying in tongues.

Tongues is our spiritual heavenly language. It is like driving the car on automatic, rather than with the gears. It is allowing the Spirit to give us the words to utter. It is God's love language when we want to praise him or we want to pray about a particular matter and don't know what to say. We allow the Spirit to pray through and in us. Tongues will usually be used in our personal prayer times, but it is also right to pray in the Spirit like this when we are gathered together and others are present to give the interpretation.

Thirdly, praying in the Spirit does not mean being impractical and doing nothing ourselves. We mustn't throw overboard all the well established aids and guidelines for prayer—prayer lists, diary, planning the prayer meeting—in favour of letting the Spirit guide us! This is as dangerous as is the opposite reaction of seeing prayer only in terms of faithfully ploughing through lists. We are human and need to be reminded through all sorts of prayer helps of the who, when, what and why of prayer. At the same time, we can pray in the Spirit—in the essential general meaning as well as in the exciting particular meaning—so that our prayers become strong, alive and effective.

What is prophecy, how do you test it, why do we need it and what should we do about responding to it in our church?

I'd like to try to answer your questions in order.

What is prophecy?

I am assuming that you are not referring primarily to the prophetic books of the Old Testament, the prophetic teaching of Jesus or the prophetic events, people and gifts referred to in the New Testament (for example: Acts 11:28; 13:1; 15:32; 21:4, 9). I mention these to remind us of the very strong prophetic theme running right through the Bible.

Bruce Yocum in his book *Prophecy* records the history of renewal movements and refers to the charismatic movements that swept through the church in the twelfth and thirteenth centuries. These brought massive changes in the church, and were marked out by healings, miracles and prophecy.

The prophetic movement is biblical, historical and contemporary. The promises of God in Joel 2:28 and Acts 2:17 are still true.

So what is prophecy? Two words are used to describe the word of God. One—*logos*—refers to the total revelation of God. We can describe the Bible as the *logos* of God. The second word used is *rhema*—and it relates to a particular word of God. Prophecy is the *rhema* of God: God's particular word, given in particular circumstances by a particular person for a particular purpose. Test that definition against the references from the Acts and I believe you will find that it fits.

It is clear from the New Testament (Romans 12:6–8; 1 Corinthians 12:7–11; Ephesians 4:11) that prophecy is a distinct gift of God's grace. The word comes from God. It is also clear that the prophetic gift must be exercised in the context of love in the local fellowship.

When the gift of prophecy is regularly and effectively exercised by the same person, the church—whether local or wider—may well recognise that God has given to that person a prophetic ministry. They may even confirm that person in the office of the prophet, though this appears to happen only rarely today.

What is the purpose of prophecy?

Given the definition above, we can go on to understand the two main purposes the New Testament gives for prophecy. First, it is given to strengthen, encourage and build up the church (1 Corinthians 14:3, 4, 12, 39). The church is built up through encouragement, guidance and inspiration. Secondly, prophecy is given to convict the unbeliever (1 Corinthians 14:24). God speaks today through prophecy, both to build up his body and to reach out to those who are not yet members of his body.

Why do we need prophecy?

People often say, 'We have the Bible—so why do we need a prophetic ministry?' May I share from our own experience?

• Sometimes the word of prophecy is a very clear word from the Bible that ministers to a direct, immediate situation. Such was Jesus' word in John 11:4: 'This illness is not unto death, but for the glory of God.'

• The word of prophecy must be in harmony with, and certainly not in contradiction to, the Scriptures. Belief in prophecy in no way undermines our faith in the final and complete authority of the Scriptures.

• The word of prophecy will be in harmony with the Bible, but may speak that more immediate word than the general teaching of the Bible can.

How should we respond to prophecy?
1 Thessalonians 5:19–21 reminds us not to 'put out the Spirit's fire, do not treat prophecies with contempt. Test everything'. We need to ponder all three commands.

Don't put out the Spirit's fire through indifference and unbelief. Don't regard either the prophetic word or the one through whom the word came with contempt, but positively test—or weigh—the word.

Here are practical guidelines.

• The prophetic word must be in harmony with the Scriptures. God will not contradict himself.

• Consider the life of the person through whom the word came. Is his a life of holiness, of personal integrity and emotional stability? Is he respected within the fellowship? Is he in good standing with the Lord and his brothers and sisters?

• Does the nature of the prophetic word relate to the situation for which it is given?

• Does the Spirit bear witness with our spirits that the word or picture is from the Lord?

I need to add something about responding to the

word of prophecy in practice. Sometimes the word is clearly a personal word to be received by one person in a small fellowship group. It may be a word of encouragement from God, through a member of the group, to someone facing a tough situation. Let that person receive the word with faith and joy and hold on to it.

Sometimes the word may be part of a number of words of prophecy or pictures, so we would need to hear the general thrust of what God is saying in a meeting. As a church, we went through a period when the emphasis in the words of prophecy which we received was a challenge to step out in faith. God persisted with that theme until we had responded. Then the character of the word changed to one of encouragement to go on in the way that the Lord was leading.

Sometimes, the word is very clear and precise and is an instruction given to the church. We need to have such words weighed by the recognised leadership, prayed over and tested, and then communicated to the congregation.

A final comment: we shall need constantly to be teaching about the gifts of the Spirit and the nature and purpose of prophecy in our churches so that members are able to respond to God's word positively and with understanding.

Can you give me some guidelines to help me understand the meaning of visions, dreams and pictures which members of our fellowship claim to receive?

People who have experienced the renewing work of the Holy Spirit can find that they are given a picture as they pray or worship privately or corporately. Maybe we should not be surprised to find that our Christianity has become more visual in a television and video age!

I want to issue a spiritual health warning to Christians who believe that having visions is an indication of maturity. Let me give you some guidelines.

• Accept the fact that God does use visions and dreams today. Surely we are promised this in Acts 2:17–18: 'I will pour out my Spirit on all people. Your sons and daughters will prophesy, your young men will see visions, your old men will dream dreams.'

• Understand that they are among the ways in which God speaks to us through prophecy today: a visual message from God. I find it significant that out of all the New Testament writers it is Doctor Luke who records the dreams and visions given by God (see Luke 1:22; Acts 9:10, 10:3, 8–9).

• Be aware of the fact that we are sinful people and recognise that dreams and visions may be incomplete, that we may not fully understand all that God wishes to reveal and that Satan can counterfeit what God promises to do (see Jeremiah 23:25, 32). It is important to check out the person receiving the dream or vision as well as its content.

• Test the visual message against and submit it to Scripture. This is essential. The dream or vision that is from God will be self-authenticating. The Holy Spirit will witness within our spirit that a message is from the Lord—if it is—but we will need also to check everything constantly against the Scriptures and to ask the Lord to reaffirm the message either through prayer or through another known and trusted member of the fellowship.

Is it wrong to ask for a sign?

It's important to ask people who want signs why they want them. Is it to bolster their faith or is it to seek God's will on some specific matter? Let me explain four things about signs from a biblical standpoint.

In some instances, signs were integral in the story of Christianity. For example, God's power and purposes in the Old Testament were accompanied by signs in an unmistakable way. There are many references to the signs and wonders done through Moses and reflected in the Psalms. Jesus' birth, death, resurrection and return, as well as his teaching and healing ministry, were or will be accompanied by signs. He himself is regarded as the greatest of all signs (see John 2:18–19).

Secondly, in complete contrast, we are warned that signs may be counterfeited and can be dangerous. There is a massive increase in the use of horoscopes, the occult, spiritism and various Satanic activities all linked with signs. People who have lost loved ones may want to seek a sign about their well-being. We are expressly forbidden to do this (Deuteronomy 18:9–13).

Thirdly, some signs are promised to us (Mark 16:17). These are signs which accompany the preaching of the gospel in power and which we are rediscovering today. They are a clear manifestation of God's power at work.

Fourthly, God knows the weakness of our faith and likes to encourage us. (Remember Gideon—Judges 6: 36–40). Clearly he is unlikely to give us a sign over matters in which he has already revealed his will through the Bible; also, he will often guide us through 'normal' channels. But there may well be other times when he will allow us to ask him for a special sign and will answer that prayer.

4

Spiritual Growth and Warfare

How can I grow in the life of the Spirit?

It's healthy to long to grow spiritually and so to be more
and more worthy of the name of Christian. Just as the
six-week-old baby weighing six pounds can grow up to
be a six foot, sixteen stone adult, so there can be
growth in the spiritual life. Physical growth is usually a
steady process with a few spurts here and there in teen-
age years; so is spiritual growth. The New Testament
describes it as walking, though it is possible to leap
forward at times—when we discover a vital new truth
about Christian living, for example.

It is important to grasp that others can't grow on our
behalf and that each of us is either going backward,
resting or growing all the time.

First, we are called to walk in the light and not in the
darkness (John 8:12; 12:35; Ephesians 5:8; 1 John 1:6).
We are not walking alone. We are walking first with the
Lord Jesus as he shows us the way, we are walking with
other Christians and we are walking in this world. As
we walk with Jesus we shall learn to keep our eyes on
him and our ears open to listen to what he is saying to
us. We shall honour him as Lord and seek to obey and

trust him. Of course, things don't always work out as smoothly as that. At times we may lose contact with him through disobedience; we may find the attractions and way of the world too strong and wander away from him. If so, we have to repent: return, put things right, confess and obey again.

Here is a good test to give ourselves, if we want to know whether we are growing spiritually or not. Can we honestly claim, before the Lord, to be walking in the light? Are there any conscious areas where we know there is darkness? As the Lord lets his searchlight of truth sweep around our lives and show us up for what we really are, and as we obediently respond, we will continue that process of growing in the Spirit.

Secondly, we are to walk in the Spirit and not in the flesh (see especially Romans 8:4–8; Galatians 5:16–25). When we speak of walking in the Spirit we are to include every aspect of the Spirit's work and ministry in our lives. Are we showing the fruit of the Spirit and open to and using the gifts of the Spirit? Are we responding to the gentle promptings of the Spirit or are we grieving and quenching the Spirit? Are we concerned with the work and mission of the Spirit? Are we rejoicing in worshipping and praying in the Spirit? Do we fill our minds with the truth of the Spirit? Are we open to the power of the Spirit? Are we seeking to maintain and preserve the unity of the Spirit in the bond of peace? Do we know the baptism of the Spirit, and are we seeking day by day to allow the Spirit to go on filling us?

I can well imagine you feeling that the New Testament should change the picture when it refers to the Christian life as a marathon or a hurdle race: it makes it sound like a long and difficult business with many obstacles to face. But it does also refer to it as walking, and walking involves putting one foot in front of the other. In my life and work, in the kitchen, the office, the school or college, the church, the factory or wherever—is Jesus lord and am I allowing his Spirit to take control of my life?

Thirdly, we are to walk by faith and not by sight (2 Corinthians 5:7). By faith, the New Testament means trust. We are called to rely upon God and not upon ourselves, our abilities, achievements or possessions. The church in the western world seems to know little about the life of faith. Our fellow-Christians in the East or the Third World, where they are forced to depend more upon God, have a real testimony to the power of God to supply their needs as they walk by faith rather than by sight. It is good to ask ourselves both personally and in our churches: On what matters, or in what areas, am I/are we especially trusting God? Is he calling me/us to trust him over some project in the fellowship? Is he calling me to step out in faith in relation to my giving? Does he want me to change my job? Is he challenging our church to reach out to a particular neighbourhood or engage in some specific Christian service? Having to trust God in particular areas helps us to learn to live by faith and grow spiritually.

Walking in the light demands holiness, repentance and obedience. Walking in the Spirit involves responding to every particular ministry of the Holy Spirit; walking by faith calls for trust in the living God. As we respond on these three levels, we will grow in the life of the Spirit.

I find it hard to listen to the Lord. What should I do?

The sales of Joyce Huggett's book *Listening to God* (Hodder & Stoughton, 1986) suggest that many other Christians are interested in this topic. Here are four guidelines that may help you to hear the Lord's voice more distinctly.

First, remember that it is your privilege and right as a Christian to hear the Lord speaking to you. In John chapter 10, where Jesus teaches that he is the good shepherd, he assures us that his sheep listen to his voice, that he calls his own sheep by name, and that they follow him because they know his voice (vs.3, 4). So be assured that God has not changed his mind, and decided to make things difficult for you.

Secondly, recognise that there may be problems and blockages in your own life that make it hard for you to hear the Lord. Sin makes it impossible to hear God (Isaiah 59:1–2); or we may be too frightened or too stubborn to hear what he would say to us, or too busy to become still before him and, like Mary, sit at Jesus' feet (Luke 10:38ff.). False expectations may also be blockages. How are you expecting the Lord to speak to you? Through a loud hailer from a passing car as you rush about? Or personally and quietly, as in a private telephone conversation for which you have made time?

Thirdly, realise the different practical ways by which the Lord speaks to us. Let me list for you some of the ways in which God speaks: through creation (Psalm 19); by visions and dreams (Acts 18:9); through the Scriptures (2 Timothy 3:16); through his Son (Hebrews 1:1–2); through his Spirit within our spirits (Acts 16:7); through the sense of God's peace (Colossians 3:15); through a particular word of knowledge or wisdom (1 Corinthians 12:8); through a still, small voice (1 Kings

19:22); through another person—such as Nathan the prophet to King David (2 Samuel 12:7). You might like to add one or two other ways. What we need to ensure is that each way is in harmony with the final revelation of God in the Bible.

Fourthly, we can learn much from stories in the Bible about people who heard God's voice. I particularly like the story of Simeon, whose name means 'listening' Luke 2:25–35) and of Samuel (1 Samuel chapter 3). The latter chapter begins with the fact that God's voice was rarely heard in the days when Eli was the priest but ends with the news that God often revealed himself to Samuel. What made the difference? Samuel had learned to expect God to speak to him and was ready to hear what the Lord had to say. More than that (vs.17, 18), Samuel had learned how to respond to the Lord once he had spoken. Although he was naturally afraid to pass on God's message (v.15), he faced those fears and, undeterred by what Eli or anyone else would think, did just that. He had learned to be faithful and obedient to what God had revealed. As a result, God knew that Samuel was a man to whom he could reveal more.

Here is an essential spiritual principle: if we respond to what God has given us, he will give us more; if we resist what God has given, then he will not trust us with further truth.

We often say, 'Listen, Lord, for your servant is speaking,' but God wants us to be those who pray, 'Speak, Lord, for your servant is listening—and is ready and willing to obey what you tell us.' If your attitude is like that of Samuel, I don't think you will have much trouble hearing what the Lord has to say to you.

My spiritual highs are almost always followed by spiritual lows. Is this the devil or normal experience?

It could be both, and it might be neither! This apparently simple question doesn't have a short answer. We are human beings, and human beings are complex people.

The different parts of our make-up all link together; the physical, emotional, mental and spiritual interrelate. It feels different having a streaming cold on a foggy November day compared with having one when relaxing in the sun during a holiday. We feel different inside when we are with a crowd of Christians praising the Lord compared with when we are facing a difficult interview before an unsympathetic committee!

We all need to discover whether our emotions, spiritual life, or physical well being is the basic cause of the trouble when we are feeling low.

Secondly, we live in days when we are too easily governed by our emotions and experiences. Our feelings can be terribly misleading. We need to learn to submit our emotions to our minds; to submit how we feel to what we know. A young Christian may not feel Christian when, in fact, he is.

Therefore, thirdly, we need to let the truth of the Bible control our minds. I may not feel that I am in Christ but the New Testament tells me that I am; that my security and position are determined by what Jesus has done for me, regardless of my feelings.

Fourthly, there are various factors that determine the state of my emotions—those factors may be physical, spiritual or psychological. We are each different. Some are highly strung, others are very calm; some are pessimists, others are optimists; and our personal make-up will affect our feelings. Some people battle constantly with depressions, others seem to be free from this for much of the time.

Fifthly, circumstances affect most people. Bereavement, loneliness, lack of money, are all powerful factors that may pull a person down.

If you read 2 Corinthians you will find that Paul frequently referred to his feelings—his fear, tiredness, restlessness and stress. In the same letter (2 Corinthians 2:14) he wrote of always being led in triumph in Christ. Jesus, in his earthly ministry, knew both joy and heaviness of heart. For as long as we live on this earth as human beings we will experience ups and downs of different sorts—sometimes the result of Satan's attacks against us, at other times the effect of our own physical, spiritual or emotional make-up and responses. What we should expect to happen is that as we become more mature in Christ we will become more stable in all our responses.

Some members of our church are planning to go away on retreat for a weekend, and I am not sure what to expect. Can you enlighten me please?

More and more people are going on retreats. There are probably a number of queries in your mind. Let me try to anticipate and respond to them.

What exactly is a retreat? Essentially a retreat is a time when we deliberately put on one side all the demands and distractions of our everyday life, make time to meet afresh with God, and allow him to touch our life in the way that he chooses. We live in such an active, noisy world that the need to slow down—or even stop and be still, to listen rather than chatter, to *be* rather than *do*, is very great.

The Bible records quite a number of retreats; men like Abraham, Joseph, David, Moses, Paul and even Jesus 'retreated' in order to meet with God at crucial times in their lives.

What will happen during a retreat? There are different kinds of retreat. These vary not only in duration (from a day to a month or so) but also according to whether they are personal or group retreats. Also, they may be based on a particular discipline, as happens for example on an Ignatian retreat.

Let me suggest a few don'ts. Don't cheat: resist the temptation to take unfinished everyday work with you. Don't worry if you find it a bit difficult to wind down and get used to periods of silence—whether they are short or long. As times goes on, the silence will become more and more valued by you and, in the stillness, you will hear the Lord speaking simply and powerfully to you from the Scriptures.

There will almost certainly be an outline programme of worship—including the Eucharist—prayers, short talks and meals. Make sure you get some good exercise. Don't forget your Bible. As you have time to read it unhurriedly, it will come alive and speak to you in an unforgettable way. In many ways don't aim to achieve anything during the weekend except to meet afresh with God—but that, after all, will be everything.

How can I get the best out of a retreat? ● You may have to resist any unexpected unwillingness to go away. You may suddenly be aware of everything you could do if you didn't go. Reject those thoughts as quickly as they come. ● Pray for the Lord's blessing on the weekend long before it happens.

● Carefully choose the Christian reading you want to take.

● Make sure you have a notebook with you to jot down what the Lord says to you. This will become a spiritual journal for you.

● Remember that life won't be the same after the retreat so don't be willing to slot back into the same noisy, active rut that you left before the weekend.

● Expect God to meet with you. The retreat will be a time when you get God's perspectives for your life and work, your marriage and home, into proper focus. You will find that your inner life will catch up with your outer world. Your heart will begin to understand what your head theoretically knows.

● Don't be anxious. You will enjoy the weekend immensely. You're in for a treat. And you will return rested, renewed and refreshed in the Lord.

Where can I find more information about retreats? If you write to the National Retreat Centre, Liddon House, 24 South Audley Street, London W1Y 5DL, they will give you details of where retreats are held and how to arrange a personal one as well as further literature and help.

Should Christians fast today?

Fasting is one of the new subjects on the Christian agenda today. People have lots of questions—both biblical and practical—to ask about it. I'm quite sure there are some circumstances in which I would have to answer, 'No,' to this question. But it will be much more helpful and positive if my reply is, 'Yes, if . . .' followed by some thoughts on the Biblical practice of fasting.

● Yes, if you have the right definition of fasting. We are not discussing a hunger strike in prison or a protest movement or any political action. The Bible's description of fasting is an abstinence from food for spiritual purposes. It is a deliberate seeking of God for a specific reason (Daniel 9:3; Acts 9:9). Richard Foster has described the benefits of fasting in these words: 'Fasting can bring a breakthrough in the spiritual realm that could never be had in any other way. It is a means of God's grace and blessing that should not be neglected any longer.'

● Yes, if the call to fast is from God and not from men only. Especially in the Old Testament, individuals and nations were called, by their leaders, to fast. The history of the Jews contained many national days of fasting (Jeremiah 36:9; Esther 4:16). But we are also told that God called his people to fast. The two outstanding occasions in the Old Testament are the Day of Atonement (Leviticus 16:29–31) and Isaiah chapter 58 which describes the true fast which God has called. Fasting was commanded in the Old Testament and presumed in the New (Matt 6:16–18). What was legally binding under the Old Covenant was to become a means of grace under the New. So we need to be sure that we are not binding ourselves into a legalism of fasting to which we are summoned by men, but entering into a means of grace to which we are called by God.

● Yes, if the reason for fasting is right. I have to confess to a sneaking feeling that we sometimes tell God he has got to bless us because we have fasted over some issue, making the fast rather than God's grace the basis of his blessing. Don't fast if you are liable to use it as a bargaining counter with God. It won't work. Enjoy a good meal, and then sort out your motives! Maybe it would help if we reminded ourselves that among the reasons for which men and women fasted in the past were the following: to seek the will and face of the Lord (2 Chronicles 20:2–3; Acts 13:2–3); to bring a note of urgency into their praying (Ezra 8:21–23); to show genuine repentance and sorrow for sin—whether personal or corporate sin—(1 Samuel 7:5–6; Nehemiah 9: 1–3; Joel 1:13–14; 2:12–18); to avert the wrath and judgement of the Lord (Deuteronomy 9:18; Jonah 3:5).

• Yes, if we are aware of the dangers of fasting. What dangers should we beware of? Jesus warned us about using fasting selfishly to be seen by men and to be thought well of: 'What a super-Christian he is' (Matthew 6:16). That surely is hypocrisy and not true spiritual humility. Also, fasting can be used to subdue the flesh. The ascetics of the fourth century believed that 'fasting insured that the stomach would not make the body boil—like a kettle—to the hindering of the soul'. Abstinence surely is right in subduing the body but this is a far cry from the spiritual purpose of fasting with which we began. Again, fasting can become formal and ritualistic, losing its original purpose. Jesus was aware of this danger (Mark 2:18–20; Luke 5:33).

• Yes, if you are seeking godly, spiritual blessings through your fasting. Seeking God through prayer and fasting brings exciting results. We may find that God will reveal his guidance; we may receive new power and fresh equipment for Christian service. Charles Finney testified to the fact that sometimes he would find himself empty of power. In such situations: 'I would set aside a day for private prayer and fasting . . . After humbling myself and crying out for help, the power would return upon me with all its freshness.' Periods of fasting can lead to a spiritual breakthrough; to growth in faith as well as spiritual alertness or physical well being (see, for example: Exodus 34:28; Acts 13:2; Luke 4:14; Mark 9:28–29; Nehemiah 9:1; Daniel 9:3; Isaiah 58:8–9).

● Yes (finally), if you will be sensible in the plans you make to fast. May I suggest that if you are not used to fasting you begin in a small way. If I can use an appropriate metaphor—don't bite off more than you can chew! There are various degrees of fasting. Abstinence involves reducing the amount you eat. Partial fasting involves missing one or two meals. Fasting proper involves missing three or more meals. Extreme fasting would be for a longer period and you would need to be clearly led by the Spirit to undertake it.

Don't be surprised if there are some aches and pains in your body, and if you are tempted to eat when you would normally expect to do so. The first meal missed is usually the hardest to forego. Don't make a show of your fasting. Do take any specific medical conditions you have (for example, diabetes) into account.

Should Christians fast today? I'm sure that many more of us would find the practice of fasting a greater means of grace if we were to allow the Spirit of God to strip away the myths that have grown up around it. I have tried to bring us back to positive, practical Biblical guidelines. Be willing to follow these, and the call of the Spirit; to enter into the fast that God chooses; then it's 'Yes' to fasting—not for its own sake, but for the resultant blessing of knowing God better.

Is there a place for penance as well as repentance when one has sinned grievously?

My dictionary defines penance as 'a sacrament in the Roman Catholic church involving the confession of sin, repentance and submission to penalties imposed, followed by absolution; any voluntary suffering to show repentance for wrongdoing'.

I would suggest that four activities have to follow any act of sin. First, there has to be confession and repentance (1 John 1:9; Luke 5:32). We need not only to admit that we have done wrong, but to turn in our hearts and minds from that sin.

Secondly, there has to be forgiveness of and redemption from sin (Ephesians 1:7). Whatever our sin—and it is clear that the Ephesians had sinned grievously (2: 1–4)—there is only one place and one way by which sin can be atoned for: through the grace of God demonstrated by the death of Christ when he shed his blood that sinners might be forgiven (Romans 5:8). We need not, cannot and must not try to work for our own salvation because that would be to insult and deny the finished, completed work of Jesus upon the Cross. The history of the church reminds us that subtle substitutes —man's works, and the church's systems of penance— can all too soon replace faith in Christ's atonement. Martin Luther's great revelation (as he read the Epistle to the Romans) which led to the Reformation, was that penance and indulgences were to be done away with as they hid the glory of the gospel of Jesus. There is no place for penance as the grounds, basis and hope for anyone to be made right with God. We are justified by faith, through grace alone.

Thirdly, there may well need to be restitution for sin. Zacchaeus (Luke 19:8) is a lovely example of a man who had sinned in his work by stealing and now realised the need to restore what he had wrongly taken. If we have hurt someone with our words, then we should seek to apologise and repair our relationship with that person. We need to give more weight to restitution of goods, reputation, relationships, as appropriate. Some people understand penance to include such acts of restitution.

Fourth and lastly, there is the need to receive the sinner back into the fellowship or into society. David (Psalm 51) prayed not only for cleansing following repentance but also for restoration. Sin affects every part of our nature, and a person may know he is forgiven but still feel emotionally and personally wounded. He may find it very difficult to forgive himself. It is here that spiritual healing needs to take place, and sometimes specific action can be part of that healing process. Some might see the discipline of penance as being involved in that healing process.

Remember the story of the Prodigal Son (Luke chapter 15)? He wanted to do penance for his grievous sin: 'Make me as one of the hired servants.' The father would not allow that at all. The son had returned with confession and repentance. The father received him by grace. It was impossible to replace the inheritance he had wasted. He needed to be restored to his father, brother and family.

We can understand why penance might seem helpful to some. There are aspects of its ministry that may need to be included in our dealing with sin, but it would be wiser to stick to Biblical terms and not run into the danger of trusting in our work when we are to trust only in Jesus for salvation.

My friend speaks of her spiritual director. It sounds a bit scary. Can you advise, please?

Many Christians are unfamiliar with the ministry of a spiritual director, but you do not need to be scared for a true spiritual director will seek only to help another Christian grow in the grace and knowledge of the Lord Jesus.

Let me clear away some common misunderstandings. Having a spiritual director is neither a status symbol nor a sign of spiritual inadequacy. They are not problem-solvers or amateur counsellors. They are not limited to one tradition of the church. While history reveals that they have emerged within the more catholic and monastic tradition of the church, their ministry is highly valued by Christians from every spiritual background.

No believer is an isolated Christian, and we are called to be 'members one of another' (1 Corinthians 12:25–27; Ephesians 4:25) in order that we minister as his body and mature in the faith. We need each other in order to grow. Such growth is pictured in the New Testament as taking a journey or fighting a war and every Christian needs to know he is travelling in the right direction or fighting in the most effective way. To this end it has been said that 'spiritual direction is not necessary for all souls, but it is very desirable for some and it can be a great help to many others . . . especially in understanding ourselves in the light of God, and growth in the life of faith and prayer' (*Dictionary of Christian Spirituality*, N. W. Goodacre, SCM, 1983, p.115).

A spiritual director will be described by some—those in the catholic tradition—as their confessor and by those in the house church movement as their shepherd.

Either way there are two major dangers to avoid—dependence on the part of the one directed and dominance on the part of the one directing. Such dangers will be avoided if it is remembered that both Christians in the relationship are alongside one another and under the guidance and direction of the Holy Spirit. There will thus be encouragement without submission and fellowship without dependence. The human relationship is to be no substitute for constant abiding in Jesus. The practice of spiritual direction may vary from a formal one-to-one relationship with a much more experienced Christian, to going away on a retreat led by a Christian minister, to the more informal *ad hoc* help and encouragement between the members of a small Christian group or cell. Whatever the method, in every way we are to grow up into Christ as head, and we usually need the encouragement and correction of other Christians.

If you would like to know more, let me recommend a super little introduction to the whole subject: *Approaches to Spiritual Direction* by Anne Long, Grove Booklet, available from most Christian bookshops.

What is 'the dark night of the soul'?

The musical 'Time', with Cliff Richard in the lead, caused at least one member of the audience to ponder deeply on the nature of light which figures prominently in this space-age production. Light has some fantastic properties which we seldom consider. Genesis reminds us that God created light. He also created darkness (Genesis 1:4) before sin ever entered the world. Thus the psalmist can speak of God's darkness and also of man's darkness (Psalm 18:11, 28) and mean two very different experiences.

The question is about a technical phrase: 'the dark night of the soul'. The phrase is attributed to St John of the Cross, but other mystics and early Christian fathers have also commented upon similar spiritual experiences. Such darkness does not refer to the results of man's sinful disobedience or to the awfulness that depression brings to the human soul. It is not associated with disappointments in life or with outward circumstances. It is a conscious, positive spiritual awareness that though God is there, you cannot relate to him or enjoy fellowship with him.

The human soul is capable of many different experiences, from overflowing exuberant joy and praise to the darkness of night with God. It is not easy to give precise biblical examples. Jesus' cry of dereliction upon the cross (Matthew 27:46; Psalm 22:1) occurred while he was bearing the sin of the world. Great men of God—like Moses and Joseph—knew times of loneliness and questioning, but we are not told exactly what they were experiencing.

We can, however, be clear that while God is light and there is no darkness of sin with him at all, there are dimensions of him that we cannot fully understand and about which we are therefore in the dark. God, in his grace and sovereignty, may well lead us through these dark times to teach us more about him. If you are going through such a tunnel not caused by any known, unconfessed sin, trust God to lead you through it. You may not know where God is, but he certainly knows about you and he asks you to reach out in the darkness in trust.

There are many difficulties in the spiritual life and 'the dark night of the soul' is a way of describing one of these. I don't think I have ever known this particular experience; should God ever choose to lead me through such a time, I would then be able to write my own description of it. The main thing is to follow the Lord in the light and trust him implicitly in the darkness, since he made both.

How can I be sure of a missionary call?

When people speak of a missionary call, they may mean (among many other possibilities): working overseas for many years with a traditional missionary society; serving for a few years with a relief agency in Africa or elsewhere; moving to a tough inner-city area of this country as a Christian social worker. A Christian in Asia might hear God's call to serve in England just as much as someone in Scotland might be called to work for the Lord in France. A missionary call can relate to many occupations and places.

People who feel called would do well to test their call by asking themselves questions such as:

● *Do I have the qualities needed for a missionary?* Am I converted and growing in Christ? Do I have a strong devotional life? Am I good in personal relationships? Am I responding from the right motives? Am I capable of doing the actual job involved? Am I physically fit and resilient? Am I mentally balanced? If married am I in full agreement with my spouse about this? Am I able to handle lower living standards? Am I able to learn other languages? Would I be happy with other church traditions? Am I able to handle loneliness and disappointment? Am I good at cultural adaptation? Am I willing to submit to others? Are there any outstanding rough edges in my personality?

● *Are my circumstances such that I am free to serve the Lord elsewhere?* Are other people so dependent upon me that I cannot leave them—i.e. elderly parents who are utterly my responsibility? Have I obtained any qualifications and finished my education at college? Have I a growing family that might well require me to stay at home?

● *Do I find the Spirit bears witness with my spirit that God is calling me* (see Acts 13:1–4; 16:10)? When God truly calls, his Spirit gives us a deepening desire to respond, and nothing else will satisfy. The inward call itself will become more and more persistent.

● *Have I received outward confirmation of the call?* Such reassuring confirmation can be both spiritual and practical. God is using dreams, visions and 'coincidences', as well as the Bible, to speak to people about his call. We also need to be very practical. If you feel that God is calling you, then seek the advice of other Christians who know you very well. Talk to your minister or elder about the possibility. As the call persists, then get in touch with the missionary society and agency that you are already committed to or the one that God is directing you to. If you have no such links, then write to two or three societies—via their personnel secretary—to ask for information and guidance about the next step. In your letter requesting help, give as much information about yourself as possible. A c.v. (*curriculum vitae*: personal profile) is helpful. The more you tell about yourself at this stage, the easier it will be for others to reply in detail to you.

A missionary call is both a very spiritual matter and a practical, down-to-earth and common sense question.

If the Lord is calling you then get to know as much as you can about other parts of the world, read the missionary literature and your daily newspaper, pray regularly and keep your heart and mind open to all that God wants to share with you at this exciting stage in your life.

What is spiritual warfare? I have heard other Christians talk about it and it sounds frightening. Should I get involved?

Different metaphors are used in the New Testament to describe the Christian life. Christians—that's us—are described as sons and daughters in the family of God, as servants in the work of God, as pilgrims on a journey, as runners in a race, as the bride of Christ united by faith to the Lord Jesus, as stones that make up a building.

We are also likened to soldiers in a fight. Because that sounds frightening some Christians might hope that it doesn't apply to them. But it does. When Jesus called us to himself and his service, to be his followers and disciples, he also enlisted us in a battle with him against evil, sin and Satan. That's spiritual warfare. We may not have heard the summons to battle, just as a football player may not have heard the referee's whistle; but that doesn't mean that the action hasn't started.

We should not be anxious, however. C. S. Lewis has reminded us that Satan should be taken seriously because of his great power, but not too seriously because he has been defeated. Jesus won the decisive battle when he died on the cross and rose again on Easter Day.

Because the question is so important, I want to answer it as fully as possible.

The reality of the spiritual battle

The key section in the New Testament is Ephesians 6:10–20. Paul has shown us in this letter that the Christian life is made up of the banquet of God's blessing, the behaviour of our daily Christian living, and the battle against Satan. There is both a feast and a fight, and we won't get one without the other.

Spiritual battle was a reality in the life of Jesus. It wasn't only in the temptations in the wilderness (Matthew chapter 4) that Jesus faced the attacks of Satan, but also at his birth when Herod sought to destroy him, during his ministry when Satan attacked him through people like Peter and Judas, and on the cross.

It is, in fact, a theme that can be traced through the Bible—from Genesis chapter 3 to Rev chapter 12 (see Joshua 5:13; Isaiah 59:17; 2 Corinthians 10:3). Every New Testament writer recognised the same truth.

Spiritual warfare is also to be found in the life of every Christian. We get a clue as to how Satan operates when we remind ourselves that Satan is the father of lies, an angel of light, and the source of all evil; so when we are faced with lies, hatred, deception, the spirit of unbelief and resentment between Christians—we are experiencing spiritual warfare. The same is true when we face the occult and spiritism. Satan also delights in harming us physically, in attacking our faith and in trying to divide Christian families and make Christians fearful and timid. He may keep in the background, using his minions and even people to do his dirty work, but he is the master-mind behind it all nonetheless. He often attacks after times of blessing and at unguarded moments; or he keeps up a continual battery so as to wear us out. But we need not be discouraged. As we have to face the reality of the spiritual battle, we can rejoice in the armour and help that is provided for us.

The resources for the spiritual battle

Ephesians 6:10–12 is a famous section. If you don't know it, mark it well in your Bible and turn to it often. You will need to have the spiritual armour on every day if you would be an effective Christian.

First, we need to take note of our position with Jesus. Paul stresses repeatedly in chapter 1 of Ephesians that we are 'in Christ'. We are united to him by faith. We are secure in him. We find all our spiritual supplies come from our living faith-union with him. The spiritual battle is not a contest that we have to fight in our own strength but a battle that we fight with the strength that God supplies. So we can rejoice in our position in Jesus.

Then we must rely on the power we receive through Jesus. Verse 10 which speaks about being strong in the Lord literally means: 'Allow the Lord to go on making you strong'—strong through the power and the gifts of the Spirit of Jesus.

In practice that means putting on the armour that God supplies (Ephesians 6:3ff.). This covers our heart, our mind and our bodies—but not our backs, so we are not to turn our backs to Satan. If we stand and resist him, we will find that he is the one who runs away. When Satan tries to accuse us of our unworthiness and to undermine our assurance, we need to have on the belt of God's truth, and the breastplate of Christ's righteousness. When he comes to hurl half-truths and doubts and lies at us, we beat them off with the shield of faith. When he contradicts the Bible, we take the sword of the Spirit which is the word of God. When we find questions arising in our minds and we begin to puzzle about our faith, we make sure we have on the helmet of salvation that covers the mind. All the time we are also to use the special weapon of praying in the Spirit—a part of the armour that Satan especially dislikes.

The reaction to the spiritual battle

It is J. B. Philips who says in his translation of the New Testament: 'We may get knocked down, but we are not knocked out.' That's so true in the spiritual battle. We may lose the odd round in the boxing match, but we shall win the fight.

We are assured of victory through the name of Jesus. The name of Jesus speaks of his victory achieved through the cross and resurrection. It is the shorthand for speaking about his character, nature and authority. The name of Jesus represents all that Jesus is, and has, and has done. If you don't know them, I suggest you find, mark and learn three verses in John's first letter— 1 John 3:8; 4:4; 5:4. They are the keys to having spiritual victory in the life of the believer. Always have the truth of Jesus' victory in mind. Never allow Satan to deceive you into believing that you are not strong enough to resist him. He may be stronger than you by yourself—but Jesus is with you and Satan therefore doesn't stand a chance.

Be willing to enter into the battle when it comes. That may mean being willing to enter into a battle in prayer for some particular answer. It may mean a period of persistent resistance against Satan's constant attacks and doubts. It may mean standing your ground on what you believe when others try to get you to compromise.

Praise the Lord for every victory won. Each victory

won will make you stronger. Every round lost will mean you have to recover ground in your Christian life, but don't panic! You won't have to go back to the starting line: you can repent, get right with the Lord and start again from where you turned away from him.

Finally, be alert for Satan's next attacks. Paul actually ends with the exhortation: 'After you have done everything . . . stand'. Don't relax or take a spiritual holiday. Don't get over anxious, either. Just stand, trusting in the Lord. Satan can't defeat you while you insist on keeping good company with Jesus. As you do that, you will be ready for his next move, and all the resources you will need will be at hand 'in Christ'.

What do people mean by binding Satan?

This spiritual practice is being established by some Christians and then copied by others, without prior searching and understanding of the Scriptures. We need to examine what the New Testament teaches and to act accordingly.

While there are a number of references to a person being bound physically, there are only two passages about the church binding and loosing (Matthew 16:19; 18:18ff.), and they are in the context of discipline in the church and agreement in prayer.

There are also only two references to Satan being bound. One (Revelation 20:2) refers to the fact that Satan will be bound for a thousand years. This is the millennium binding, which in itself raises a different set of questions! The other passage is in Matthew 12:29 (cf. Mark 3:27).

It is on this saying of Jesus that we have built the

practice of binding Satan. What did Jesus mean? He was involved in controversy with the Pharisees after he had healed a demon-possessed man who was also blind and dumb. The Pharisees believed that Jesus had healed through Beelzebub, the prince of demons. Jesus refuted this charge and went on to explain about the power encounter between the Kingdom of God and the Kingdom of Satan, and to say that before the strong man's (i.e. Satan's) house could be entered, the strong man would have to be tied up: his power would have to be limited.

The New Testament makes it very clear that Jesus, through his death and resurrection (1 John 3:8; Colossians 2:14, 15), has already bound Satan and limited his power, so Christians have been given power and authority over him and all his demonic, evil allies. We can't bind Satan and we don't need to, because Jesus has already done it. Our part is to:

● Recognise what Satan's position in the world is since Christ died on the cross and rose again. He is the prince of this world; he is prowling around seeking to destroy; he still blinds people's eyes to prevent them seeing and understanding the good news (see, for example, 2 Corinthians 4:4; 1 Peter 5:8). (My book *Prayer Changes People* has a chapter on victory over Satan which might be helpful.)

● Receive and use the power and authority that Jesus has given to his disciples to be effective in the world and victorious over evil spirits and demons. While we do not bind Satan, because Jesus has already bound him, we are now able, in the name of Jesus, to bind (limit and curb) his power and to cast out evil spirits and demons in people's lives. To use a simple illustration: we can deal with a broken fuse in our house and not be afraid of touching electricity once we know someone else has thrown the main switch off. In the same way, Jesus has dealt with the main evil power so we can now deal with the evil spirits. These we are able to bind, knowing they will be bound in heaven; we are also able to loose (set free) people who have been bound, knowing they will be set free in heaven.

● Respond personally to the New Testament commands about the devil. We are to have on the whole armour of God; to resist, to give no place to the devil and to be aware of his devices (Ephesians 6:10; James 4:7; 1 Peter 5:9; 2 Corinthians 2:11). We are to cast out demons, commanding them in the name of Jesus to leave (Luke 9:1; 10:17–20). We are to be watchful (see 1 Corinthians 16:13): watchful for the return of Christ; watchful also for those times when we may be in error through building a doctrine on other people's experiences and habits rather than on the Bible. Christ has already, by his words and works, bound Satan. We are to resist the devil, be firm in our faith, persistent in prayer and consistent in the work and mission to which Jesus has called us.

Has the renewal movement led to an unhealthy interest in Satan and the occult?

The simple answer is, 'No!' However, let me add more that may be helpful.

First, a spiritual vacuum exists—and has existed—in any life where Jesus is not known as saviour and lord. People may try to ignore this emptiness or they might fill it with fake substitutes; among such will be the activities of Satan and the manifestations of occult (or spiritually hidden) practices. It is rather like a garden where, because no flowers or vegetables are planted, weeds take root and grow up. These are not new phenomena. Long ago, Moses confronted the magicians of Egypt, and warned the people of Israel against spiritualist practices (Deuteronomy 18:9–14) and Paul included sorcery or witchcraft in the list of works of the flesh (Galatians 5:20).

Secondly, the renewal movement has made Christians more aware of these realities and more able to respond to and overcome them. We are experiencing the power encounter—between the forces of evil and the might of the Spirit of God.

The Lord Jesus more than anyone else displayed the power of God in his ministry and confronted the forces of evil and the devil. Just as he aroused the activity of Satan when he ministered in the fulness of the Spirit, so Christians today who are filled with the Spirit become more aware of the reality of evil and the subtlety of the occult.

Of course, there can be dangers. Some Christians—especially new, immature or unstable believers—can be either too fearful of the occult or fascinated by the demonic. Others, ignorant of the Bible's teaching about the person and work of Satan, 'see' demons and evil spirits at every turn of the road. As these people grow in their Christian understanding through daily reading of the Bible, and as they are open to the inspiration of the Spirit, they will mature in their spiritual judgement.

Neither they nor any other Christian need be frightened of this new awareness of the forces of evil and darkness. For God has left us the lovely promise—in 2 Timothy 1:6–8—that we have not been given a spirit of fear, but of power and love and self-control. He has also assured us (1 John 4:1ff.) that we are able to test the spirits and know their true origin.

The renewing work of the Spirit has enabled many of us to understand rightly the work of evil in its various forms, and has also equipped us by the power of the Spirit to overcome it in the victorious name of Jesus.

Can demons harm Christians?

Demons are real. They are referred to as evil spirits in the New Testament (Matthew 9:32–34; 11:18; 12:43–45; 15:22–28; 17:18), and they are part of the evil forces under Satan's control. Jesus took them seriously, but he did not fear them or become obsessed with them. We are to have the same attitude.

I believe that demons or evil spirits can harm Christians. They can take up residence in any part of our personality—our body, mind, emotions or spirit. They express themselves in such ways as uncleanness, lying, distorted speech or physical manifestations (Mark 5:1–13; Acts 16:18; James 2:19).

The most important thing for us to know about demons is that we have the victory over them in the name of Jesus. The majority of Christians will never have personal dealings with demons (but if you do, it is essential to ask for help and counsel from your minister or pastor). Some Christians allow the demons entry into their lives through disobedience and involvement with various forms of the occult or spiritism. But every Christian can enter into the victory we have in Jesus.

Christ has defeated and destroyed all the works of Satan through his death and resurrection. His power is immeasurably greater than Satan's, and we can claim the promises in Colossians 2:15; 1 John 3:8; 4:4; 5:4.

Demons are real and can harm Christians but, as we abide in Christ and give no place and opportunity to Satan, as we daily put on our spiritual armour (Ephesians 6:11–12) and enjoy our position in Christ, they will have to flee at the name of Jesus.

Should demon-expulsion be carried out by specially trained people?

The description of the disciples in the Gospels and the great commission given to the church would suggest that this ministry of driving out demons is one that every disciple can be engaged in (Luke 9:1; 10:17; Mark 16:17). In theory that is true and it should be the target to aim at. However, experience and practice tell us that only specially trained and properly authorised people should minister in such situations. This is for four reasons.

First, the Christian church has not yet reached a point where we have a commonly accepted definition of demon-expulsion. We are not agreed as to what demonisation or deliverance ministry is. There is a lot more work to be done to bring us to a point where there can be an agreed understanding and therefore a harmonised discipline.

Secondly, great care needs to be exercised in diagnosing demon-possession or the extent of demonisation. For example, some aspects of inner healing—when someone may release the hurt of pain that has been hidden for years—can at times be very similar to the physical manifestation of demonisation. Again, the ministry to the Christian and the non-Christian who is demonised will differ.

Thirdly, our make-up and personalities are complex. We can do harm both by ministering deliverance to those who don't need it and by not ministering it to those who do. We need to remember that Satan is described as 'an angel of light', and he can deceive in such areas of ministry.

Fourthly, we must remember that most churches have official policies of discipline and authorisation operating in these areas of demonisation or exorcism. The fact of this discipline is right, following some horrific and tragic events in the 1970s where such ministry was sadly misapplied. From an Anglican position, the Archbishops of Canterbury and York have laid down clear guidelines.

Does this, therefore, mean that all lay people who have been involved in this ministry have been wrong? I don't believe so, but we need to work at two aspects of this issue.

First, we need to ensure that all who minister in local churches, especially following the visits and teaching of John Wimber, do so under the authority and with the authorisation and knowledge of their own minister. He will be responsible to the bishop for all that happens in his parish.

Secondly, I personally long to see a revision of the Archbishop's guidelines so that official recognition is given in the Church of England—and maybe in the other churches and denominations as well—to all that God by his Spirit has been doing in the last five years. This is a clear case of the structures of the church needing to catch up with what the Spirit is doing and saying wherever individuals and churches are making way for him to act.

What is the Spirit of God saying to his church at this time?

I was strongly tempted to ignore this question, and I'm sure that readers will understand why. I have no authority and certainly no prophetic gift to state categorically what the sovereign Lord is saying by his Spirit to his church at this time. I would be more than foolish to rush in where even angels fear to tread.

However, I believe there are comments that I can make in answer to this question that may help us to know what the Spirit is saying to the church.

First, remember that the Lord speaks to individuals, groups of Christians, as well as to his whole church. Thus you may not feel able to know what the Lord is saying to others, but you should be able to hear what the Lord is saying to you. 'Let him (or her) that has ears, hear what the Spirit is saying . . .'

Secondly, it is helpful to realise that God often reveals his purposes gradually and progressively. This was true in Old Testament times. It was true of the Lord's teaching methods for his disciples. Do you recall Jesus saying to His disciples: 'I have much more to say to you, more than you can now bear. But when he, the Spirit of truth, comes, he will guide you into all truth' (John 16:12–13)? God seems to reveal his will step by step.

Thirdly, we must recall, as we think about the future, that God has already made some things very clear. We have been taught about the sure and certain return of Jesus. We have been given some signs about the end times (see Matthew chapter 24 and Mark chapter 13) and God is not going to change his mind on what he has already said. Thus a time of accountability and judgement will come. There will come a time when it will be too late for people to respond to the Gospel.

Fourthly, I believe that God is longing that we do not just hear his word with our minds, but that we allow the heart of God to touch our hearts, and for our hearts to beat more fully in time with God's. God's heart, surely, is a heart of compassion for the lost, the needy, the unsaved, the prisoners, the Third World, the under-privileged, the blind, the naked. His heart beats for others, and God is speaking to his church about our service to others, our costly involvement with others, our evangelism in a world that is lost, and our vision for the whole of God's world, and not just part of it.

God's heart is also a heart of holiness and purity, and it is a heart that is grieved by the sin, compromise and indifference among his people. It is a heart that hurts at the materialism, greed and secularism that so often is found in the church. It is a heart that calls his people to repentance and a new depth of obedience.

God's heart is a heart of love for all his children. He longs for all his children to recognise and receive each other, rather than to divide and to destroy each other. It is a heart that yearns for the unity of his body, and longs that we shall love our brothers and sisters in Christ who differ from us, as he loves each of us.

God's heart is a heart that keeps on beating. It does not stop. It will persist, and God's Spirit is urging his church to persist and to persevere in the things to which the Lord has called us. How easy it is for his body to give up when the going gets tough! But I sense that the Lord is urging us not to give way, or to break away, but to make way for his Spirit to enable us to continue in the work to which God has called us.

Above all, God's heart is a heart that longs for his glory: 'My glory I will not give to another.' He has been saddened when men's idols have held sway in his church rather than his Son the Lord Jesus Christ. He has made Jesus head of his church for his glory, and God's heart longs for that day when all his body will acknowledge that Jesus Christ is Lord.

I am only one person among millions to whom the Lord is speaking. I hear only a fraction of what the Spirit is saying to his church. I share what I hear.

Lastly, can I ask you again: Are you personally willing to listen to and hear what the Spirit of God is wanting to say to you individually? Will you respond in your life and church? Will you go on making way for the Spirit?

USEFUL BOOKS

There are many books relating to renewal. I have included in this list some of these.

Bax, Josephine. *The Good Wine:* Spiritual Renewal in the Church of England, Church House Publishing, 1986.

Bennett, Dennis. *Nine O'clock in the Morning*, Kingsway, 1971.

Bittlinger, Arnold. *Gifts and Graces*, Hodder and Stoughton, 1967.

Bridges, Donald and Phypers, David. *More Than Tongues Can Tell*, Hodder and Stoughton, 1972.

Carey, George. *The Church in the Market Place*, Kingsway, 1984.

Cassidy, Michael. *Bursting the Wineskins*, Hodder and Stoughton, 1983.

Cole, Michael. *He is Lord*, Hodder and Stoughton, 1987.

Cole, Michael. *Prayer Changes People*, Marshall, 1986.

Cole, Michael. *Living by the Cross*, Marshall, 1988.

Dobson, James. *Emotions, Can You Trust Them?*, Hodder and Stoughton, 1982.

England, Dr. Ann ed. *We Believe in Healing*, Highland Books, 1986.

Foster, Richard. *Celebration of Discipline*, Hodder and Stoughton, 1980.

Foyle, Marjory. *Honourably Wounded*, MARC Europe, 1987.

Glennon, Jim. *Your Healing is Within You*, Hodder and Stoughton, 1978.

Glennon, Jim. *How Can I Find Healing?*, Hodder and Stoughton, 1984.

Goodacre, N. W. *Dictionary of Christian Spirituality*, SCM, 1983.

Gunstone, John. *A People for His Praise*, Hodder and Stoughton, 1978.

Harper, Michael. *None Can Guess*, Hodder and Stoughton, 1971.

Harper, Michael. *As at the Beginning*, Hodder and Stoughton, 1965.

Harper, Michael. *Walk in the Spirit*, Highland Books, 1985.

Higton, Tony. *That the World May Believe*, Marshall, 1986.

Huggett, Joyce. *Listening to God*, Hodder and Stoughton, 1986.

Maries, Andrew. *One Heart, One Voice*, Hodder and Stoughton, 1985.

MacDonald, Gordon. *Restoring Your Spiritual Passion*, Highland Books, 1987.

MacDonald, Gordon. *Ordering Your Private World*, Highland Books, 1985.

McClung, Floyd. *The Father Heart of God*, Kingsway, 1985.

Kendrick, Graham. *Worship*, Kingsway, 1984.

Perry, John. *Christian Leadership*, Hodder and Stoughton, 1983.

Pytches, David. *Come, Holy Spirit*, Hodder and Stoughton, 1985.

Pytches, Mary. *Set My People Free*, Hodder and Stoughton, 1987.

Sandford, John and Paula. *The Elijah Task*, Logos International, 1977.

Sandford, John and Paula. *The Transformation of the Inner Man*, Bridge Publishing, 1982.

Sandford, John and Paula. *Healing the Wounded Spirit*, Bridge Publishing, 1985.

Schlink, Basilea. *Repentance—the Joy-filled Life*, Lakeland, 1968.

Slosser, Bob. *Miracle in Darien*, Logos International, 1979.

Smail, Tom. *The Forgotten Father*, Hodder and Stoughton, 1980.

Taylor, Jack. *The Hallelujah Factor*, Highland Books, 1985.

Virgo, Terry. *Restoration in the Church*, Kingsway, 1984.

Wagner, Peter. *Your Spiritual Gifts*, Regal Books, 1982.

Walker, Andrew. *Restoring the Kingdom*, Hodder and Stoughton, 1985.

Walker, Tom. *Renew Us by Your Spirit*, Hodder and Stoughton, 1982.

Watson, David. *One in the Spirit*, Hodder and Stoughton, 1973.

Watson, David. *You Are My God*, Hodder and Stoughton, 1983.

Watson, David. *Discipleship*, Hodder and Stoughton, 1981.

Wimber, John. *Power Evangelism*, Hodder and Stoughton, 1985.

Wimber, John. *Power Healing*, Hodder and Stoughton, 1986.

Yocum, Bruce. *Prophecy*, Servant Books, 1976.

INDEX OF QUESTIONS

155

Section Two: The Local Church

Section Four: Spiritual Growth and Warfare